DEAD SEA SCROLLS

DEAD SEA [SCROLLS]

AN EXHIBITION OF SCROLLS AND ARCHAEOLOGICAL OBJECTS
FROM THE COLLECTION OF THE ISRAEL ANTIQUITIES AUTHORITY

וידעו כי אני יהוה

**ART GALLERY OF NEW SOUTH WALES
IN ASSOCIATION WITH THE ISRAEL ANTIQUITIES AUTHORITY**

Published by the
Art Gallery of New South Wales
© 2000 Art Gallery of New South Wales

National Library of Australia
Cataloguing-in-publication data:

Dead Sea (Scrolls)

Bibliography
ISBN 0 7347 6307 7

1. Israel. Rashut ha-'ati.kot – Library –
Exhibitions. 2. Dead Sea scrolls –
Exhibitions. 3. Manuscripts, Hebrew –
Jerusalem – Exhibitions. 4. Qumran
community – Exhibitions. 5. Qumran Site
(West Bank) – Exhibitions. I. Israel.
Rashut ha-'ati.kot. II. Art Gallery of New
South Wales. III. Title: Dead Sea Scrolls.
English and Hebrew. Selections 2000.

296.1550749441

Copy editor **Anna Macdonald**
Catalogue design **Analiese Cairis**
Production **The Design Department,
Art Gallery of New South Wales**
Film **Spitting Image, Sydney**
Printing **The Pot Still Press, Sydney**

Photography
Landscapes by Edmund Capon and
Richard Johnson.
All other photographs by Clara Amit,
Tsila Sagiv and Mariana Salzberger
© Israel Antiquities Authority, Jerusalem.

To avoid religious connotations, the
Christian Era has been renamed
throughout the catalogue: the
abbreviations BC (before Christ) and
AD (*anno Domini*, in the year of our Lord)
have been replaced by BCE (Before the
Common Era) and CE (Common Era).

Art Gallery of New South Wales
acknowledges the previous publication
Scrolls from the Dead Sea produced in
conjunction with exhibitions held at the
Library of Congress, Washington, 1993;
the New York Public Library, 1993; M.H.
de Young Memorial Museum, San
Francisco, 1994.

Exhibition dates
Art Gallery of New South Wales, Australia
14 July–15 October 2000
National Gallery of Victoria, Australia
early 2001
Auckland Museum, New Zealand
late 2001

Distribution
Art Gallery of New South Wales,
Art Gallery Road, The Domain,
Sydney, NSW 2000, Australia

Front cover
War Rule scroll (catalogue 9)

6 **SPONSOR'S STATEMENT**

7 **FOREWORD** EDMUND CAPON, ART GALLERY OF NEW SOUTH WALES

9 **INTRODUCTION** AMIR DRORI, ISRAEL ANTIQUITIES AUTHORITY

11 **THE CULTURAL HERITAGE OF THE DEAD SEA SCROLLS** MICHAEL E. STONE

14 **TREASURES FROM THE JUDAEAN DESERT** AYALA SUSSMANN AND RUTH PELED

25 **THE PALAEO-HEBREW AND JEWISH SCRIPTS** ADA YARDENI

28 **CONSERVATION OF THE DEAD SEA SCROLLS** PNINA SHOR

29 **PUBLICATION OF THE DEAD SEA SCROLLS** EMANUEL TOV

30 **ABOUT THIS CATALOGUE** AYALA SUSSMANN AND RUTH PELED

DEAD SEA SCROLLS

32 FROM THE SCROLL CAVES

EXODUS

PSALMS

PSEUDO-EZEKIEL

NAHUM COMMENTARY

COMMUNITY RULE

DAMASCUS DOCUMENT

SOME TORAH PRECEPTS

THANKSGIVING PSALMS

WAR RULE

CALENDRICAL DOCUMENT

ENOCH

PHYLACTERY

82 FROM THE QUMRAN RUIN

108 **GLOSSARY**

115 **CONTRIBUTORS**

116 **SELECTED BIBLIOGRAPHY**

SPONSOR'S STATEMENT

Westfield is proud to be the principal sponsor of the *Dead Sea Scrolls* exhibition at the Art Gallery of New South Wales, National Gallery of Victoria and the Auckland Museum.

This is the first time that these extraordinary documents, discovered by chance in the Judaean Desert and including the earliest known biblical scrolls, have been brought to Australia and New Zealand. The exhibition therefore provides a wonderful opportunity for Australasians, and visitors from overseas, to see the famous scrolls for themselves.

The exhibition includes not just the scrolls but a range of relics from the Khirbet Qumran site and, so, offers a unique insight into the origins of Judaism and Christianity and, indeed, Western civilisation.

On behalf of Westfield, I hope you enjoy this fascinating experience.

Frank Lowy AC, Chairman, Westfield Holdings Limited

FOREWORD

The Dead Sea scrolls are a collection of fragmentary manuscripts of humble presence but extraordinarily powerful evocation. The remains of these texts hint at the values, structures and sensibilities of Jewish communities in the pre-Christian era upon which so much of our common ethos is now founded. As such they are of fundamental significance for the history of Judaism and for the emergence of Christianity. Thus it is that they inevitably touch upon our most sensitive and deep-seated values and instincts and have provoked extraordinary levels of debate and emotive controversy. As the meaning of the scrolls gradually unfolds it is not only the issue of interpretation that is the cause of conflicting views, for such is their significance that the question of ownership inevitably arises. Who wrote the scrolls? Who were these people that inscribed, albeit in uncertain and indistinct terms, attitudes towards moral and social values and structures which have become pertinent to the foundations of Western civilization? There is a sense of universality about the Scrolls – their presence and image seem to touch and to be relevant to us all. Perhaps it is that we suspect, and perhaps even need, their affirmation of the values which, seemingly instinctively, have contributed so much to our basic morality.

The interest in this the first exhibition of the Dead Sea Scrolls to be held in Australia and New Zealand tends to confirm, through the sheer interest generated, that sense of universal ownership; that these fragments of thoughts and details dating back some two thousand years or more are not just moments of passing curiosity but relics that have a bearing upon us and our values today. An exhibition of and fresh debate around the scrolls are, therefore, especially timely events to be held in association with one the great global manifestations of our time, the Olympic Games in the year 2000.

This exhibition will, inevitably, pose more questions than it answers, but in doing so it will further the interest in and the debate surrounding these relics of universal history. Hopefully, though, some of the most fundamental and most frequently asked questions can be answered: firstly, just how old are the scrolls? That may now be answered beyond dispute: they were written between from the 3rd century BCE to the 1st century CE. Secondly, who wrote them? Whilst current scholarship still tends to the view that the scrolls were written by the Essenes – a pious separatist Jewish sect which sought to re-establish their community with an adherence to the most traditional and conservative of social and religious dimensions – there remains a degree of uncertainty about this contention. And thirdly, what do the scrolls mean? That is a question of immense scope, but the three categories of texts found have at least given some specific dimension to that question. Approximately one-third of the scrolls represent the texts of the Hebrew Bible, that is the Old Testament; the second group comprises apocryphal material which may be best described as part of the literary heritage of the Jewish people of the time; and the third group is so-called sectarian material which relates to the life and times of the people who actually wrote the texts, and has, therefore, the most valuable documentary evidence. Scrolls from all three categories of material are included in this exhibition.

This exhibition has been organised by the Israel Antiquities Authority and we must express our great appreciation to its director, Amir Drori, and to the staff of the Authority who have worked so diligently on our behalf; above all I record my thanks to Ruth Peled, Ayala Sussmann, Pnina Shor and Hava Katz.

The Dead Sea Scrolls exhibition is one of the major components of the Sydney 2000 Olympic Arts Festival and we express our thanks to SOCOG for its support of this unique project. To our sponsors for the Australasian tour our appreciation to Westfield for its invaluable contribution. The world of Dead Sea Scrolls scholarship is spread around the world and many scholars have been of great help to us in organising this exhibition. I wish to express my special thanks to Professor Lawrence H. Schiffman, Professor Emanuel Tov, Professor Michael Stone, Professor Geza Vermes and Professor Hanan Eshel for their help, advice and, in some cases, participation. I also express my own special thanks to the Israeli Consul-General in Sydney, Mr Effi Ben-Matityahu, who played such a crucial role in bringing the Dead Sea Scrolls to Australia and whose humour and enthusiasm for the project has ensured its success. In Australia we have received constant support and help from many people particularly Professor Alan Crown and Rachael Kohn. The design of the exhibition has been sensitively undertaken by Richard Johnson, and the catalogue and exhibition graphics by Analiese Cairis. In the Gallery my special thanks to the Director of Exhibitions, Anne Flanagan in managing the project and to Liz Gibson who has prepared and organised an impressive and mandatory range of seminars, conferences and public programmes. Finally I acknowledge the co-operation of the National Gallery of Victoria and the Auckland Museum for their participation in the exhibition tour.

Edmund Capon, Director, Art Gallery of New South Wales

8

INTRODUCTION

It is with great pleasure that the Israel Antiquities Authority has agreed to lend a representative selection of original manuscripts of the Dead Sea Scrolls, together with related artefacts from the excavations at Qumran, to tour in Australasia, coinciding with the 2000 Olympic Games in Sydney.

The Israel Antiquities Authority has, since its establishment, promoted the preservation of this astounding cache of ancient manuscripts for future generations, and has supported an intense research and publication programme which is now approaching completion. A major objective has also been the presentation of the scrolls, accompanied by the story of their discovery, to as wide a public as possible.

Thanks to the diligent and able research of scores of scholars, we have in recent years improved our understanding of the significance of the scrolls, though they are not yet fully comprehended. Nevertheless, the unrivalled interest and eager enthusiam that the scrolls have generated have encouraged us to facilitate their exhibition.

It is to this end that a representative showing of biblical and sectarian scrolls seemed a fitting endeavour. Although the scrolls were uncovered more than half a century ago, they have not ceased to generate excitement and interest, either among scholars or with the general public. This exhibition displays a judicious selection of scrolls revealing the deeply rooted convictions of the communities they served. The addition, in this exhibition, of manuscripts reflecting on similarities and emphasising, yet again, the common roots of the monotheistic religions well suits the beginning of a new millennium.

The *Dead Sea Scrolls* exhibition features 12 scrolls, some of substantial size, some mere fragments, as well as a selection of archaeological artefacts excavated in Qumran and its environs in the Judaean Desert. Written from the third century BCE, but chiefly in the first century BCE and first century CE, the scrolls contain fragments of all the books of the Hebrew Bible. Especially significant was the discovery of fragments of the Apocrypha, which previously had been known only in Greek and Latin. Now, for the first time, the scrolls give us the Hebrew and Aramaic originals.

This catalogue relates the story of the scrolls' discovery and illuminates their historical and archaeological context: the scroll texts are accompanied by transcriptions, translations and explanations; the various theories concerning the nature of the Qumran community, its identity and its theology are explored; and the challenges facing modern researchers as they struggle to reconstruct the texts and contexts from the thousands of fragments that remain are discussed. The exhibition enables visitors to understand the nature and working methods of archaeologists, historians, linguists, paleographers and conservators.

The present exhibition is the product of a fruitful collaboration between the Art Gallery of New South Wales, the National Gallery of Victoria, the Auckland Museum and the Israel Antiquities Authority. Special thanks are due to Edmund Capon, Director of the Art Gallery of New South Wales, who so willingly endorsed the exhibition proposal and its tour to Melbourne and Auckland.

Amir Drori, Director, Israel Antiquities Authority

CULTURAL HERITAGE OF THE DEAD SEA SCROLLS MICHAEL E. STONE

The Dead Sea Scrolls are a subject of apparently endless fascination, both for scholars and the public at large. To appreciate the exhibition of the scrolls being mounted in Australia, it is necessary to understand this attraction. What is it about the Dead Sea Scrolls that makes any discovery or controversy between experts news around the world? Why is the subject so engrossing that, after more than half a century, thousands of articles and books have been published on it? What other field in the study of the ancient world has aroused such a vigorous and sustained attention?

It is fortuitous that an exhibition of ancient Hebrew manuscripts is to be opened in Sydney in 2000, at the time of the Olympic Games. These two great streams, the Judaeo-Christian and the Greek, have been the major tributaries flowing into western culture. The ideas and perceptions developed in the Land of Israel in the last millennium BCE combined with the extraordinary efflorescence of the human spirit that was classical Greece to produce a rich cultural mixture, of which Australia, with all its variety of cultural heritages, partakes in many forms. It is in the context of this broad picture that the Dead Sea Scrolls should be viewed.

At the barren site of Qumran, on the north-west corner of the Dead Sea, tens of thousands of fragments of manuscripts were discovered in a dramatic series of finds that began in 1947 and continued through the 1950s. These parchment and papyrus documents survived time and circumstance. Myriad fragments were pieced together into parts of about 800 compositions, most written in Hebrew, some in Aramaic and relatively few in Greek. The process of fitting together the pieces of what might be characterised as the greatest jigsaw puzzle of all time has gone on since the first discoveries. Scholars are still shifting the positions of some fragments, reassigning others, and deciding that yet others are part of a still unrecognised work.

There has been a number of finds of manuscripts in the Judaean Desert, surrounding the Dead Sea, in the past half-century and the Dead Sea Scrolls are only one of them. However, with few exceptions, apart from those discovered at Qumran all the manuscripts have been legal or administrative documents, carried with them by refugees from the almost incessant turmoil that enveloped the Holy Land during the centuries before and after the turn of the era. What is unique and distinctive about the find at Qumran is that virtually all the Dead Sea Scrolls are literary manuscripts and they are religious writings of various types. They include all the books of the Hebrew Bible but Esther, a number of Jewish apocryphal writings from the Second Temple period which were known from other sources, and very many previously unknown documents. All the writings are Jewish and, moreover, rumours that fragments of Gospels were found are not correct.

What is it, then, that makes them so fascinating? It is, of course, that they come from a period of history and a place on earth that played a particularly important role in the development of the religious and intellectual culture in which we live. This period has been studied by Jews and Christians for two millennia, but new manuscript finds, of which the Dead Sea Scrolls are the most prominent, demand that reconsideration of the subject.

In the course of the past 150 years or more, scholars have been engaged in the task of learning about the Jewish background of the New Testament. No longer is it enough to accept the New Testament as a unique and unparalleled revelation. It has become evident that Jesus of Nazareth was a Jew, the society in which he lived and preached was Jewish, and the first adherents to his teaching were fellow Jews. Scholars undertook the task of studying the Judaism from which Jesus arose and the religious and intellectual life of the age during which he preached. This motivation, above all others, has fuelled research into the Dead Sea Scrolls. How immensely exciting, then, it is to have an unparalleled corpus of Jewish literature from the period of the life of Jesus in the original languages. The Dead Sea Scrolls have raised such sustained and widespread interest, both scholarly and lay, precisely because they are what they are: Jewish religious books, written before, during and after the life of Jesus, in Judaea, where Jesus preached and died.

When the history of Dead Sea Scrolls scholarship is examined, it becomes evident that the role played by Jewish scholars was different from that of Christian scholars. For Jews, the Dead Sea Scrolls provide extraordinarily rich information for a period of their past that was pivotal and from which the Jewish tradition itself preserved few writings. However, between 1948 and 1967, the Dead Sea Scrolls were for the most part in Jordan, a state then at war with Israel. Even after the Six Day War of 1967, many of the older organisational structures were left in place and it was not until 1990 that Jewish scholars gained equal access to the Dead Sea Scrolls. Today, the field of Dead Sea Scrolls research is characterised by close cooperation between Jewish and Christian scholars, to mutual benefit.

The scrolls are particularly significant because, although often extremely fragmentary, they are in the original Hebrew and Aramaic languages. The evidence they give has not been transmitted through the filters of later Jewish and Christian orthodoxy; it is immediate and unchallengeable in its originality and must be taken into account by scholars for that reason. Although the great jigsaw puzzle has almost been completed, the task ahead is even more challenging than assembling the puzzle, more difficult than the job of decipherment, translation and initial interpretation. It is the integration of this newly available data into the body of accumulated knowledge about Judaism in the ancient age. The picture that will emerge of the religious, intellectual and political history of the Jews from that time will be crucial for understanding the development of rabbinic Judaism and the origins and growth of Christianity.

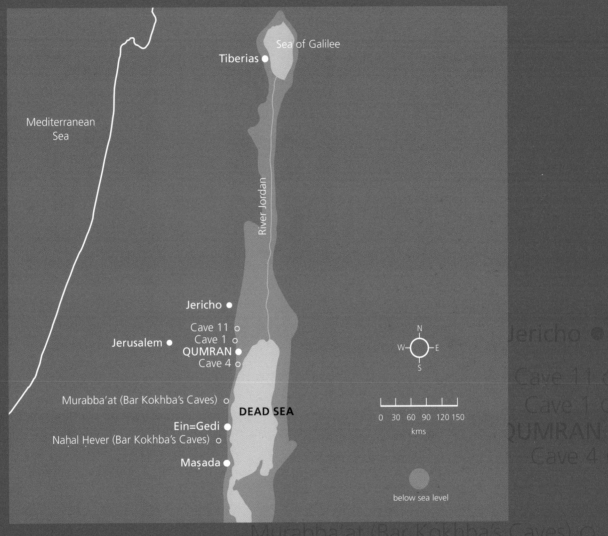

Mediterranean
Sea

Sea of Galilee

Tiberias ●

River Jordan

Jericho ●

Cave 11 ○
Cave 1 ○
Jerusalem ● QUMRAN ●
Cave 4 ○

Murabba'at (Bar Kokhba's Caves) ○

DEAD SEA

Ein=Gedi ●
Naḥal Ḥever (Bar Kokhba's Caves) ○

Maṣada ●

N
W ○ E
S

├──┼──┼──┼──┼──┤
0 30 60 90 120 150
kms

below sea level

TREASURES FROM THE JUDAEAN DESERT
AYALA SUSSMANN AND RUTH PELED

Ancient Hebrew scrolls that were accidentally discovered in 1947 in the Judaean Desert by a Bedouin boy have kindled popular enthusiasm as well as serious scholarly interest over the past half a century. The source of this excitement is what these Dead Sea Scrolls reveal about the history of the Second Temple period (520 BCE–70 CE), particularly from the second century BCE until the destruction of the Second Temple in 70 CE, a time of crucial developments in the crystallisation of the monotheistic religions.

One discovery led to another, and 11 scroll-yielding caves and a habitation site eventually were uncovered. Since 1947, the site of these discoveries – the Qumran region (the desert plain and the adjoining mountainous ridge) and the Qumran site – have been subjected to countless searches. The first trove found by the Bedouin in the Judaean Desert consisted of seven large scrolls from what is now called Cave 1. The unusual circumstances of the find, on the eve of Israel's War of Independence, obstructed the initial negotiations for the purchase of all the scrolls. Shortly before the establishment of the State of Israel, Professor E.L. Sukenik of the Hebrew University acquired three of the scrolls from a Christian Arab antiquities dealer in Bethlehem. The remaining four scrolls reached the hands of Mar Athanasius Yeshua Samuel, Metropolitan of the Syrian Jacobite Monastery of St Mark in Jerusalem. In 1949, he travelled to the United States with the scrolls, but five years went by before the prelate found a purchaser.

On June 1, 1954, Mar Samuel placed an advertisement in *The Wall Street Journal* offering "The Four Dead Sea Scrolls" for sale. The advertisement was brought to the attention of Professor Sukenik's son, Yigael Yadin, who had recently retired as chief of staff of the Israel Defence Forces and reverted to his primary vocation, archaeology. With the aid of intermediaries, the four scrolls were purchased from Mar Samuel for US$250,000. The scrolls that had eluded the father were now at the son's disposal.

The seven scrolls from Cave 1, now on exhibit to the public in the Shrine of the Book in Jerusalem's Israel Museum, are Isaiah A, Isaiah B, the Habakkuk Commentary, the Thanksgiving Scroll, the Community Rule (or the Manual of Discipline), the War Rule (or the War of the Sons of Light Against the Sons of Darkness) and the Genesis Apocryphon, the last being in Aramaic.

ARCHAEOLOGICAL INVESTIGATIONS

The Caves At least a year elapsed between the discovery of the scrolls in 1947 and the initiation of a systematic archaeological investigation of the Qumran region. The northern Dead Sea area, the location of Qumran, became and remained part of Jordan until 1967. The search for scroll material rested in the hands of the Bedouin, who ravaged the Cave 1 site. Early in 1949, the cave site was finally identified by the archaeological authorities of Jordan. The director of the Jordanian Antiquities Department, G. Lankester Harding, undertook to excavate Cave 1 with Père Roland de Vaux, a French Dominican priest who headed the École Biblique in Jerusalem. Exploration of the cave, which lay a kilometre north of Wadi Qumran, yielded at least 70 fragments, including bits of the original seven scrolls. This discovery established the provenance of the purchased scrolls. Also recovered were archaeological artefacts that confirmed the scroll dates suggested by palaeographic study. The Bedouin continued to search for scrolls, as these scraps of leather proved to be a fine source of income. Because Cave 1 had been exhausted by archaeological excavation, the fresh material that the Bedouin were offering proved that Cave 1 was not an isolated phenomenon in the desert and that other caves with manuscripts also existed. The years between 1951 and 1956 were marked by accelerated activity in both the search for caves and the archaeological excavation of sites related to the manuscripts. An eight-kilometre-long strip of cliffs was thoroughly investigated. Of the 11 caves that yielded manuscripts, five were discovered by the Bedouin and six by archaeologists.

Some of the caves were particularly rich in material. Cave 3 preserved two oxidised rolls of beaten copper (the Copper Scroll), containing a lengthy list of real or imaginary hidden treasures – a tantalising enigma to this day. In Cave 4, 15,000 fragments from at least 600 composite texts were found. Cave 11, the last manuscript cave discovered, in 1956, provided extensive documents, including the Psalms Scroll (catalogue 2), an Aramaic *Targum* of Job, and the Temple Scroll. Yigael Yadin acquired the Temple Scroll in 1967; it is now housed with the first seven scrolls in the Shrine of the Book at the Israel Museum. All the remaining manuscripts – sizable texts, as well as minute fragments – are stored in the Rockefeller Museum building in Jerusalem, the premises of the Israel Antiquities Authority.

Khirbet Qumran (The Qumran Ruin) De Vaux gradually realised the need to identify a habitation site close to the caves. Excavating such a site could provide clues that would help to identify the people who deposited the scrolls.

The ruins of Qumran lie on a barren terrace between the limestone cliffs of the Judaean Desert and the bed of a fossil lake along the Dead Sea. The excavations uncovered a complex of structures, 80 by 100 metres, preserved to a considerable height. De Vaux regarded the structures as neither military nor private but rather communal in character. Nearby were remains of burials. Pottery uncovered was identical to that found in Cave 1 and confirmed the link with the nearby caves.

Following the initial excavations, de Vaux suggested that this site was the wilderness retreat established by the Essene sect, which was alluded to by ancient historians. The sectarians inhabited neighbouring locations, most likely caves, tents and solid structures, but depended on the centre for such communal facilities as stores of food and water. Excavations conducted in 1956 and 1958 at the neighbouring site of Ein Feshkha proved it to be the agricultural adjunct of Qumran.

Khirbet Qumran

HISTORY

First Temple period	850–586 BCE
Second Temple period	520–70 CE
First Jewish Revolt	68–70 CE

Literary Milestones

c. sixth century BCE	Canonisation of the Torah (Pentateuch), the first of the three major divisions of the Hebrew Bible
c. fourth century BCE	Canonisation of the Nevi'im (the Prophets), the second of the three major divisions of the Hebrew Bible
c. mid-third century BCE	Completion of the Septuagint (translation of the Pentateuch into Greek)
c. 200 BCE–100 CE	Apocryphal and apocalyptic literature
c. 40–50 CE	Beginnings of the New Testament
c. 90 CE	Canonisation of the Ketuvim (Hagiographa), the third of the three major divisions of the Hebrew Bible
c. 200 CE	Mishnah edited by Rabbi Judah the Prince

Key Figures

Hillel	c. 60 BCE–c. 9 CE
Philo of Alexandria	c. 30 BCE–45 CE
Jesus of Nazareth	c. 4 BCE–29 CE
Pontius Pilate, procurator of Judea	26–36 CE
Josephus Flavius	c. 38–100 CE

Hasmonean Dynasty

Judas Maccabeus	166–160 BCE
Jonathan	160–142 BCE
Simeon	142–134 BCE
John Hyrcanus	134–104 BCE
Aristobulus	104–103 BCE
Alexander Jannaeus	104–76 BCE
Salome Alexandra	76–67 BCE
Aristobulus II	67–63 BCE
Hyrcanus II	63–40 BCE
Antigonus II	40–37 BCE

Herodian Dynasty

Herod the Great	37–4 BCE
Archelaus	4 BCE–6 CE
Herod Antipas	4 BCE–39 CE
Herod Philip	4 BCE–34 CE
Agrippa I	41–44 CE
Agrippa II	50–c. 92 CE

Political and Military Events

586 BCE	Babylonians destroy Jerusalem; beginning of Babylonian exile
538 BCE	Cyrus, ruler of Persia, permits exiles to return to Judea
333 BCE	Alexander the Great extends Greek rule to Palestine and Egypt
323 BCE	Alexander's empire divided into three parts: Antigonids in Macedonia, Seleucids in Syria and Ptolemies in Egypt
301 BCE	Ptolemies' rule over Judea begins
198 BCE	Seleucids' rule over Judea begins
168 BCE	Hasmonean revolt
164 BCE	Temple purified by Judas Maccabeus
63 BCE	Rome occupies Jerusalem
37 BCE	Herod conquers Jerusalem
6–41 CE	Judea, Samaria and Edom placed under procurators
44–66 CE	Rule of the procurators
66 CE	Revolt against Rome
c. 68 CE	Roman legions destroy the Qumran settlement
70 CE	Roman legions conquer Jerusalem
73 CE	Maṣada falls to Rome

Dating of the scrolls The discovery of the Dead Sea Scrolls caused heated controversy in scholarly circles over their age and the identity of the community they represented.

Professor Sukenik, after initially defining the provenance of the scrolls as the Second Temple period, recognised their special significance and advocated the theory that they were remnants of the library of the Essenes. At that time, however, he was vociferously opposed by a number of scholars who doubted the authenticity of the texts. Today, scholarly opinion regarding the timespan and background of the Dead Sea Scrolls is anchored in historical, palaeographic and linguistic evidence, corroborated firmly by carbon-14 datings. Some manuscripts were written and copied in the third century BCE, but the bulk of the material, particularly the texts that reflect on a sectarian community, are originals or copies from the first century BCE; a number of texts date from as late as the years preceding the destruction of the site, in 68 CE, at the hands of the Roman legions.

THE ESSENES

The origins of the Qumran sect are thought by some to be in the communities of the *Hasidim*, the pious anti-Hellenistic circles formed in the early days of the Maccabees. The *Hasidim* may have been the precursors of the Essenes, who were concerned about growing Hellenisation and strove to abide by the Torah.

Archaeological and historical evidence indicates that Qumran was founded in the second half of the second century BCE, during the time of the Maccabean dynasty. A hiatus in the occupation of the site is linked to evidence of a huge earthquake. Qumran was abandoned at about the time of the Roman incursion of 68 CE, two years before the collapse of Jewish self-government in Judaea and the destruction of the Temple in Jerusalem in 70 CE.

The chief sources of information for the history of this fateful timespan are the Qumran scrolls and the excavations, but earlier information on the Essenes was provided by their contemporaries: Josephus Flavius, Philo of Alexandria and Pliny the Elder. Their accounts are continuously being borne out by the site excavations and study of the writings.

The historian Josephus relates the division of the Jews of the Second Temple period into three orders: the Sadducees, the Pharisees and the Essenes. The Sadducees included mainly the priestly and aristocratic families, the Pharisees constituted the lay circles, and the Essenes were a separatist group, part of which formed an ascetic monastic community that retreated to the wilderness. The exact political and religious affinities of each of these groups, as well as their development and interrelationships, are still relatively obscure and are the source of widely disparate scholarly views.

The crisis that brought about the secession of the Essenes from mainstream Judaism is thought to have occurred when the Maccabean ruling princes, Jonathan (160–142 BCE) and Simeon (142–134 BCE), usurped the office of high priest (which included secular duties), much to the consternation of conservative Jews; some of them could not tolerate the situation and denounced the new rulers. The persecution of the Essenes and their leader, the "Teacher of Righteousness", probably elicited the sect's apocalyptic visions. These included the overthrow of the "Wicked Priest" of Jerusalem and of the evil people and, in the dawn of the Messianic Age, the recognition of their community as the true Israel. The retreat of these Jews into the desert would enable them "to separate themselves from the congregation of perverse men" (Community Rule 5:2).

A significant feature of the Essene sect is its calendar, which was based on a solar system of 364 days, unlike the common Jewish calendar which was lunar and consisted of 354 days. It is not clear how the sectarian calendar was reconciled, as was the normative Jewish calendar, with the astronomical time system (see Calendrical Document, catalogue 10). The sectarian calendar was always reckoned from a Wednesday, the day on which God created the luminaries. The year consisted of 52 weeks, divided into four seasons of 13 weeks each, and the festivals consistently fell on the same days of the week. A similar solar system was long familiar from pseudepigraphic works. The sectarian calendar played a weighty role in the schism of the community from the rest of Judaism, as the festivals and fast days of the sect were ordinary workdays for the mainstream community, and vice versa. The author of the Book of Jubilees accuses the followers of the lunar calendar of turning secular "days of impurity" into "festivals and holy days" (Jubilees 6: 36-37).

The Essenes persisted in a separatist existence through two centuries, occupying themselves with study and a communal way of life that included worship, prayer and work. It is clear, however, that large groups of adherents also lived in towns and villages outside the Qumran area.

The word "Essene" is never distinctly mentioned in the scrolls. How, then, can we attribute either the writings or the sites of the Judaean Desert to the Essenes? The argument in favour of this ascription is supported by the tripartite division of Judaism referred to in Qumran writings (for example, in the Nahum Commentary), into Ephraim, Menasseh and Judah, corresponding to the Pharisees, the Sadducees and the Essenes. As the Essenes refer to themselves in the scrolls as Judah, it is clear who they regarded themselves to be. Moreover, their religious concepts and beliefs as attested in the scrolls conform to those recorded in contemporary writings and stand in sharp contrast to those of the other known Jewish groups.

In most cases, the principles of the Essene way of life and beliefs are described by contemporaneous writers in language similar to the descriptions found in the scrolls. Customs described in ancient sources as Essene – such as the probationary period for new members, the strict hierarchy practised in the organisation of the sect, their frequent ablutions, communal meals – are echoed in the scrolls. Finally, the location of the sect is assigned to the Dead Sea area by the Roman historian, Pliny the Elder.

Diversity of opinions Although this evidence is accepted by the majority of scholars in identifying the Essenes with the Qumran settlement and the manuscripts found in the surrounding caves, some scholars remain unconvinced. Some propose that the site was a military garrison or even a winter villa. The scrolls are viewed as an eclectic collection, neither necessarily inscribed in the Dead Sea area nor sectarian in nature, perhaps even the remains of the library of the Temple in Jerusalem. Other scholars view the texts as the writings of forerunners or even followers of Jesus – Jewish Christians – who still observed Jewish law.

Ancient sources provide us with diverging reports regarding the living environment of the Essene communities: Philo stated that they lived in small villages, Josephus wrote that they were scattered in various settlements, whereas Pliny referred to a separate Essene settlement located near the Dead Sea.

The central structures at the site of Qumran could have functioned as a centre for the activities of

The excavations at Khirbet Qumran.

a community during the day. However, only a small number of individuals could have lived there. Due to finds in the vicinity of the site, it has been surmised by many that most of the community members lived in neighbouring caves, tents and huts which were linked to the site by a network of paths.

It is feasible that the isolated location of the Dead Sea would lure such a group as the Essenes, as it represented an eschatological paradise, an abode of purity and a haven where they could cut themselves off from the impure. Only at the End of Days would they return from the desert, "to camp in the Desert of Jerusalem" (War Rule 1: 2–3) and wrest Jerusalem from the hands of the wicked.

A sectarian's day began before dawn with the recitation of prayers, hymns and benedictions. Phylacteries found in the excavations (see catalogue 12) give reason to assume that these were worn during prayers. Meals were communal and probably accompanied by blessings – "They shall eat in common and bless in common and deliberate in common" (Community Rule 6: 2–3) – outlining a life reminiscent of a monastic community.

Hardly any mention is made either by historians or in the sect's writings of the daily occupations and livelihood of the inhabitants. It is obvious, however, that such a group would have functioned as a self-sufficient unit. True evidence of agriculture comes from the site of Ein Feshkha, a mere three kilometres away. Remains of date pits and palm fronds were found at both sites, as well as in the caves. Recent excavations have also revealed the production of date honey.

Sheep and cattle were raised in the area, as evidenced by the wealth of parchment found, both used and unused. This indicates tannery activity, which can probably be linked to the pools and channels uncovered at the site. Pieces of linen and wool, sheep shears, spindle whirls, mats and baskets are all evidence of production of textiles and weaves. A potters' workshop, including a kiln, substantiates the assumption that pottery was produced at the site. Scribal work could have occupied a number of Qumranites, as well – the inkwells recovered are proof of local scribal activity.

No doubt a certain measure of market economy was locally practised; the large number of coins recovered could represent wages received for work outside the community. Within the community's bounds, a communal ownership of property and means was, no doubt, the rule:

"But when the second year has passed, he shall be examined, and if it be his destiny, according to the judgment of the Congregation, to enter the community, then he shall be inscribed among his brethren in the order of his rank for the Law, and for justice, and for the pure Meal; his property shall be merged and he shall offer his counsel and judgment to the Community" (Community Rule 6:20–23)

THE QUMRAN LIBRARY

The writings recovered in the Qumran environs have restored to us a voluminous corpus of Jewish documents dating from the third century BCE to 68 CE, demonstrating the rich literary activity of Second Temple period Jewry. The collection comprises varied documents, most of them of a distinct religious bent. The chief categories represented are biblical, apocryphal or pseudepigraphical, and sectarian writings. The study of this original library has demonstrated that the boundaries between these categories are far from clear-cut.

The biblical manuscripts include what are probably the earliest copies of these texts to have come down to us. Most of the books of the Bible are represented in the collection. Some books are extant in a large number of copies; others are represented on scraps of parchment. The biblical texts display considerable similarity to the standard Masoretic (received) Text. This, however, is not always the rule, and many texts diverge from the Masoretic. For example, some of the texts of Samuel from Cave 4 follow the Septuagint, the Greek version of the Bible translated in the third to second centuries BCE. Indeed, Qumran has yielded copies of the Septuagint in Greek.

The biblical scrolls in general have provided many new readings that facilitate the reconstruction of the textual history of the Old Testament. It is also significant that several manuscripts of the Bible, including the Leviticus Scroll, are inscribed not in the Jewish script dominant at the time but in the ancient palaeo-Hebrew script.

A considerable number of apocryphal and pseudepigraphic texts are preserved at Qumran, where original Hebrew and Aramaic versions of these Jewish compositions of the Second Temple period were first encountered. These writings, which are not included in the canonical Jewish scriptures, were preserved by different Christian churches and transmitted in Greek, Ethiopic, Syriac, Armenian and other translations.

Some of these are narrative texts closely related to biblical compositions, such as the Book of Jubilees and Enoch (catalogue 11), whereas others are independent works. Apparently, some of these compositions were treated by the Qumran community as canonical and were studied by them.

The most original group of writings from Qumran are the sectarian ones, which were practically unknown until their discovery in 1947. An exception is the Damascus Document, which lacked a definite identification before the discoveries of the Dead Sea area. This widely varied literature reveals the beliefs and customs of a pietistic commune, probably centred at Qumran, and includes rules and ordinances, biblical commentaries, apocalyptic visions and liturgical works generally attributed to the last quarter of the second century BCE and onwards.

The "rules", the collections of rules and instructions reflecting the practices of the commune, are exemplified by the Damascus Document (catalogue 6), the Community Rule (catalogue 5), and Some Torah Precepts (catalogue 7). Here, we witness a considerable corpus of legal material (*halakhah*) that has much in common with the rabbinic tradition preserved at a later date in the Mishnah. The *halakhah* emerging from the sectarian writings seems to be corroborated by the sectarian *halakhah* referred to in rabbinic sources.

The biblical commentaries (*pesharim*), such as the Habakkuk Commentary, the Nahum Commentary (catalogue 4) and the Hosea Commentary, are attested solely at Qumran and grew out of the sect's eschatological presuppositions. The Scriptures were scanned by the sect for allusions to current and future events. These allusions could be understood only by the sectarians themselves, because only they possessed "eyes to see" – their distinct eschatological vision. Liturgical works figure prominently among the sectarian manuscripts at Qumran, due to the centrality of prayer in this period. The Thanksgiving psalms (*Hodayot*) are of two types: those characterised by a personal tone, attributed by some to the "Teacher of Righteousness", and the communal type, referring to a group.

Many more compositions deserve mention, but this brief survey demonstrates the major role played by the Dead Sea Scrolls in our understanding of this pivotal moment in Jewish history.

Scholars in the 1950s, studying fragments
of the Dead Sea Scrolls.

The ancient Hebrew script, also known as the palaeo-Hebrew script, is one of the offshoots of the Phoenician script. It was the exclusive Hebrew script of the First Temple period from about 850 to 586 BCE, in both the Judaean and the Israelite kingdoms.

In the wake of the destruction of the First Temple (586 BCE) and the ensuing exile, Hebrew lost its prominent, singular status in favour of Aramaic, which had become the official language of the Persian empire. In the post-Exile period, in the Diaspora and in Judaea as well, the cursive Aramaic script gradually replaced the ancient Hebrew script for secular writing as well as for holy scriptures. (Jewish tradition maintains that Ezra the Scribe established that custom on returning from the Babylonian exile.) The palaeo-Hebrew script, however, was not completely abandoned. Although of limited use, it apparently held a high nationalistic and religious status and was used particularly in priestly circles, as well as in times of nationalistic strife or revival. The palaeo-Hebrew script appears on a variety of materials: stone, pottery, coins and papyrus. However, the major finds in this script from the late Second Temple period are from Qumran. Palaeo-Hebrew characters are used for about a dozen biblical scrolls and, interestingly, are employed for writing the Tetragrammaton, the four-lettered divine name, and occasionally in manuscripts otherwise written in the Jewish script.

The major changes that occurred in the palaeo-Hebrew script were the levelling of the height of the letters of the alphabet (the Jewish script underwent a similar process) and changes in the stance of the letters. Of chronological significance are the changes in the length of the downstrokes and in the inclination of the letters towards the ensuing letters. However, a proper cursive style did not evolve in palaeo-Hebrew script, possibly because of its limited use.

Of special interest from Qumran is the Exodus Scroll (catalogue 1), written in the palaeo-Hebrew script. The Exodus fragments were dated on palaeographical grounds (their script resembling the script on Hasmonean coins) to the late second or early first century BCE. The almost uniform direction of the downstrokes, sloping to the left, indicates an experienced, rapid and rhythmic hand.

The Jewish script is one of the offshoots of the late formal Aramaic cursive script. It emerged when the latter split into local scripts following the fall of the Persian empire in the second half of the fourth century BCE.

A group of dated documents, the latest from 335 BCE, found at Wadi Daliyeh along the Jordan Valley, is in the late Aramaic script. It bears affinity with the script of the earliest Qumran scroll fragments (4QSam[b]), which may be regarded as a link between the Aramaic and the Jewish scripts. Certain late Aramaic letter forms prevail in documents written in early Jewish script.

The earliest dated document in the Jewish script is from Wadi Murabba'at, dated to the second year of the emperor Nero (55/56 CE). Because no Qumran document yet published bears an explicit date, Qumran scholars must rely on historical, archaeological and palaeographical data. Thus, the earliest documents from Qumran have been dated to the late third or early second century BCE. Formal development of the letters is reflected, for example, in the straightening of the curved strokes, resulting in the formation of angular joins which give the Jewish bookhand its square appearance. Another characteristic is the regularity of the writing, which is a result of the suspension of the letters on horizontal guidelines (not attested in Aramaic documents written in ink). At this early stage of independent development, the letters in the Jewish script were not yet adorned with ornamental additions, except for the inherited serifs in several letters. The distinction between thick horizontal and thin vertical strokes, characteristic of the late Aramaic scripts, is still evidenced in the earliest documents from Qumran – and occasionally even in later documents – but is not typical of the Jewish script.

Three main periods in the development of the Jewish script are distinguished: the Hasmonean period (167–30 BCE), the Herodian period (30 BCE–70 CE) and the post-Herodian period (70–135 CE). The majority of Qumran documents belong to the first two periods, although there are some earlier fragments as well. The variety of handwritings testifies to the activity of scores of scribes. It is reasonable, therefore, to believe that some of the documents found in the caves of Qumran came from other places.

Fragments of Pseudo-Ezekiel (catalogue 3) include fine examples of Hasmonean script. The Prayer for King Jonathan (Alexander Jannaeus, 104–76 BCE), dated to the first quarter of the first century BCE, exhibits a variety of letter forms in bookhand as well as semi-cursive and cursive hands.

A significant increase in ornamental elements in the letters – in the form of independent additional strokes – is evidenced in the Herodian period, together with the levelling of the height of the letters. Examples of the Herodian script here include the Psalms Scroll (catalogue 2), the Nahum Commentary (catalogue 4) and the Calendrical Document (catalogue 10). It is also characterised by the crystallisation of different script styles, such as the calligraphic bookhand (later to develop into the ornamental script style used for Torah scrolls) and the standard cursive script style that prevailed in Judaea during the late Herodian and the post-Herodian periods. It went out of use at the end of the Bar Kokhba Revolt (132–135 CE). This cursive style served for official as well as literary documents: an early form appears, for example, in one of the manuscripts of Enoch from Qumran (catalogue 11), and its later forms are attested on ossuaries and inscriptions from the Herodian period, on *ostraca* from Maṣada dating to the end of the Herodian period, and in documents from the late first and early second centuries CE. The Jewish bookhand continued to exist and developed many script styles in widely dispersed Jewish communities. The Hebrew script used today is its modern descendant.

Styles of Hebrew Script

1 Palaeo-Hebrew
8th century BCE

2 Jewish Script
Temple Scroll

3 Oriental
(includes handwritings used in
the Near East and North Africa)
9th–10th centuries CE

4 Sefardi
13th–15th centuries CE

5 Ashkenazi
14th–15th centuries CE

1	2	3	4	5	
	א	א	א	א	alef
	ב	ב	ב	ב	bet
	ג	ג	ג	ג	gimmel
	ד	ד	ד	ד	dalet
	ה	ה	ה	ה	he
	ו	ו	ו	ו	vav
	ז	ז	ז	ז	zayin
	ח	ח	ח	ח	ḥet
	ט	ט	ט	ט	tet
	י	י	י	י	yod
	כ	כ	כ	כ	kaf
	ך	ך	ך	ך	final kaf
	ל	ל	ל	ל	lamed
	מ	מ	מ	מ	mem
	ם	ם	ם	ם	final mem
	נ	נ	נ	נ	nun
	ן	ן	ן	ן	final nun
	ס	ס	ס	ס	samech
	ע	ע	ע	ע	ayin
	פ	פ	פ	פ	peh
	ף	ף	ף	ף	final peh (feh)
	צ	צ	צ	צ	ẓade
	ץ	ץ	ץ	ץ	final ẓade
	ק	ק	ק	ק	qof
	ר	ר	ר	ר	resh
	ש	ש	ש	ש	shin
	ת	ת	ת	ת	tav

CONSERVATION OF THE DEAD SEA SCROLLS PNINA SHOR

The constant, arid climate of the Dead Sea area, which is about 400 metres below sea level, was probably the major factor contributing to the preservation of documents through two millennia until the removal of the first scrolls from their hiding place in 1947 and their transfer to Jerusalem. Indeed, the drastic change in climatic conditions rendered them vulnerable to damage. Jerusalem, at about 800 metres above sea level, is of an extremely different climate from that of the Judaean Desert.

The scrolls were at first unknowingly handled in inappropriate methods and an uncontrolled environment. Moreover, in the first years, adhesive tape used in joining fragments and covering cracks caused irreversible damage. The scrolls were then moistened and flattened loosely between plates of window glass and sealed with adhesive tape.

The ageing of the adhesives and the pressure of the glass caused the skins to darken – to the extent that some of the texts are no longer legible – and the edges to gelatinise.

In the 1970s, a team of conservators from the Israel Museum began to treat some of the fragments: the adhesive tape and some of the stains were removed, the fragments were reinforced and the glass plates were replaced with cardboard. It became evident, however, that the degree of deterioration that had set in called for more urgent steps to be taken.

In 1991, a climate-controlled storeroom and laboratory for the conservation and preservation of the scrolls were set up by the Israel Antiquities Authority in the Rockefeller Museum building in Jerusalem, where four conservators have since been engaged in full-time efforts to preserve the scrolls.

Detailed descriptions of the condition of the fragments are recorded; these include photography and mapping of each of the fragments, no matter how minuscule. However, the most time-consuming task is the removal of the adhesive tape: it is loosened by water-based adhesives, a poulticing agent and drops of solvent. Once the remains are removed, oils and other stains are cleaned, and the back of the scroll is reinforced wherever necessary. This operation cannot be standardised and each of the thousands of extant fragments needs individual consideration. The preserved fragments are arranged on acid-free cardboards, attached with hinges of Japanese tissue paper and stored in solander boxes in the climate-controlled storeroom.

While preparing the scrolls for exhibition, a new housing system was devised. The fragments are sewn between two layers of polyester net stretched in acid-free mounts. These in turn are enclosed in a frame made of polycarbonate plates. Unfortunately, the process of ageing cannot be halted. We are striving to slow it down with as little intervention as possible, employing reversible methods. The conservation and preservation procedures are extremely lengthy and costly. But the Dead Sera Scrolls are a universal cultural heritage which must be saved for future generations.

PUBLICATION OF THE DEAD SEA SCROLLS EMANUEL TOV

Since 1947, tens of thousands of inscribed fragments of parchment – pieces from almost a thousand compositions, mainly literary documents – were found in the Judaean Desert, particularly the Qumran area. The majority, fragments of some 800 documents, come from the caves around Qumran, while remnants of more than 150 documents and compositions were found in other locations in the Judaean Desert – for example, Naḥal Ḥever, Wadi Murabbaʼat, Naḥal Ṣeʼelim and Maṣada. Several compositions were preserved in large scrolls, while others are single-page documents.

Well-preserved texts included long ones, such as the Isaiah Scroll (732cm) from Cave 1 and the Temple Scroll (884.5cm) from Cave 2. Most of the compositions, however, are fragmentary. The pieces were sorted into hundreds of groups, and scholars attempted to assemble comprehensible texts. A tiny fragment of Chronicles (4Q118) represents all that has been preserved of the 65 biblical chapters of 1–2 Chronicles. But a more difficult and more representative case is that of the Pseudo-Ezekiel literature, for which there are scores of fragments representing an unknown percentage of an unknown number of compositions.

The texts from the Judaean Desert include more than 200 scrolls of biblical compositions, several hundred varied literary compositions, and a limited number of non-literary documents. These documents, in Hebrew, Aramaic and Greek, are of crucial importance for the study of the early exegesis of the Bible, its textual transmission, and the Hebrew and Aramaic languages, as well as the literature and the history of ideas of the Second Temple period.

Full publication of this complex corpus of documents has taken longer than was envisaged by the small team assigned in the 1950s to publish the newly found texts. Publication includes identification, decipherment, transcription, reconstruction, annotation on matters of palaeography, texts, and translation. All these elements, accompanied by facsimiles of the texts, are included in the official edition, published by Clarendon Press: *Discoveries in the Judaean Desert* (*DJD*). Twenty-seven volumes have already appeared; another 12 volumes are scheduled to be published in this series, along with an index volume and a complete concordance. Sixty scholars from nine countries, representing North America, Israel and Europe – expanded from the original eight persons in the 1950s – are engaged in this project.

In addition, photographs of all fragments have been available since 1993 in a microfiche edition by E. Tov with the collaboration of S.J. Pfann: *The Dead Sea Scrolls on Microfiche: A Comprehensive Facsimile Edition of the Texts from the Judaean Desert*.

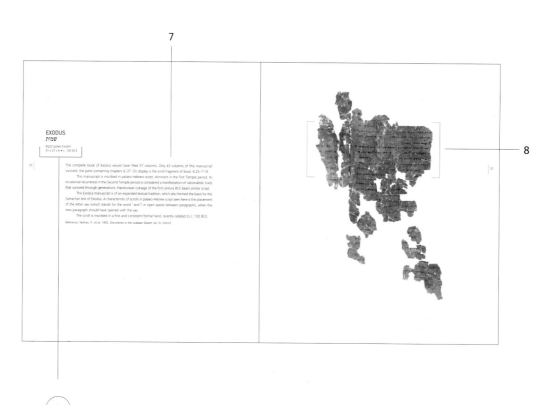

EXODUS
שמות

4Q22 (paleo Exod^m)
31 x 21 cm • c. 100 BCE

The complete book of Exodus would have filled 57 columns. Only 43 columns of this manuscript survived, the parts containing chapters 6–37. On display is the scroll fragment of Exod. 6:25–7:19.

This manuscript is inscribed in palaeo-Hebrew script, dominant in the First Temple period. Its occasional recurrence in the Second Temple period is considered a manifestation of nationalistic traits that survived through generations. Hasmonean coinage of the first century BCE bears similar script.

This Exodus manuscript is of an expanded textual tradition, which also formed the basis for the Samaritan text of Exodus. A characteristic of scrolls in palaeo-Hebrew script seen here is the placement of the letter vav (which stands for the word "and") in open spaces between paragraphs, when the new paragraph should have opened with the vav.

The scroll is inscribed in a fine and consistent formal hand, recently redated to c. 100 BCE.

Reference: Skehan, P., et al. 1992, *Discoveries in the Judaean Desert*, vol. IX, Oxford.

---

1 — (1)

2 —— EXODUS

3 —— שמות

4 —— 4Q22 (paleo Exod^m)

6 —— 31 x 21 cm • c. 100 BCE

5

ABOUT THIS CATALOGUE

This catalogue was compiled by Ayala Sussmann and Ruth Peled with additional entries by Tamar Schick and Donald T. Ariel.

The catalogue is divided into two main sections. The first, "From the Scroll Caves", describes the 12 scroll fragments included in the exhibition. The second section, "From the Qumran Ruin", presents artefacts excavated at the nearby Qumran ruin in addition to scroll jars from the caves.

The curatorial descriptions of the scrolls include the following elements:

1. An exhibit number.
2. A translated name for the scroll (for example, Nahum Commentary).
3. The name of the scroll in Hebrew.
4. The scroll's classification number. The traditional notation generally includes some or all of the following information: the number of the cave in which the fragment was uncovered; the location of the cave; the number assigned to the overall fragment; an abbreviated name; and the specific fragment number (for example, the classification number 4QpHos° would indicate Cave 4, Qumran, Pesher Hoshe'a, fragment a).
5. An approximation of the period in which the scroll was copied.
6. Measurements of the fragment, in centimetres.
7. A description of the scroll. Reference to the major publication of the fragment, as well as its transcription and translation, are located at the foot of the entry.
8. Markings around the scroll photographs. These assist the reader in locating the transcribed portions.
9. On the pages following the image: a translation, as well as a transcription into Hebrew script of a portion of the text. Translated and transcribed text enclosed in brackets indicates letters, words or passages reconstructed by the editor; in parentheses are additions he deemed necessary for fluency.

The second section of the catalogue, "From the Qumran Ruin", describes the archaeological artefacts. They are organised by material, such as pottery, wood, leather and textiles. Brief introductions and captions describe the materials and their uses.

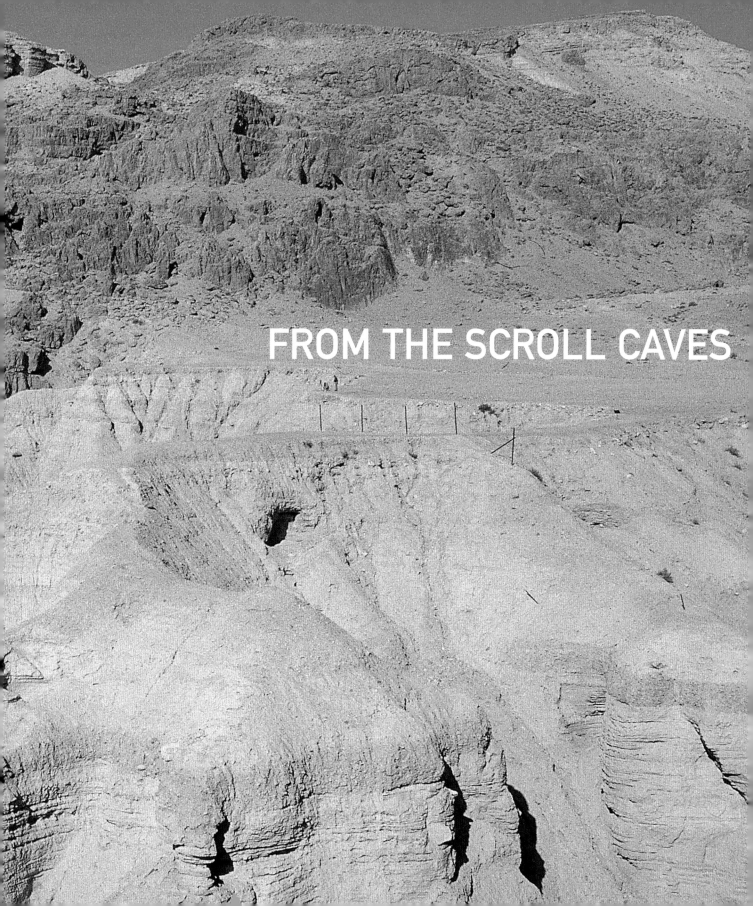

FROM THE SCROLL CAVES

EXODUS
שמות

4Q22 (paleo Exodᵐ)
31 x 21 cm • c. 100 BCE

The complete book of Exodus would have filled 57 columns. Only 43 columns of this manuscript survived, the parts containing chapters 6–37. On display is the scroll fragment of Exod. 6:25–7:19.

This manuscript is inscribed in palaeo-Hebrew script, dominant in the First Temple period. Its occasional recurrence in the Second Temple period is considered a manifestation of nationalistic traits that survived through generations. Hasmonean coinage of the first century BCE bears similar script.

This Exodus manuscript is of an expanded textual tradition, which also formed the basis for the Samaritan text of Exodus. A characteristic of scrolls in palaeo-Hebrew script seen here is the placement of the letter *vav* (which stands for the word "and") in open spaces between paragraphs, when the new paragraph should have opened with the *vav*.

The scroll is inscribed in a fine and consistent formal hand, recently redated to c. 100 BCE.

Reference: Skehan, P., et al, 1992, *Discoveries in the Judaean Desert*, vol. IX, Oxford.

[   ]   [הוא אהרון ומשה אשר ^{26:6}   2

[אמר יהוה] להם הוציאו את בנ[י] ישראל מארץ מצרים על   3

[צבא]תם ²⁷הם המדברים אל פרעה מלך מצרים להוציא את בני   4

[ישראל] ממצרים הוא משה ואהרון ²⁸ויהי ביום דבר   5

[יהוה] אל משה בארץ מצרים ²⁹   6

[ידבר] יהוה אל משה לאמר אני יהוה דבר אל פרעה מלך מצרים   7

[את כל א]שר אני דובר אליך ³⁰ויאמר משה לפני יהוה   8

[הן אני] ערל שפתים ואיך ישמע אלי פרעה ^{1:7}ויאומר   9

[יהוה] אל משה ראה נתתיך אלהים לפרעה ואהרון אחיך יהיה   10

[נביאך] ²אתה תדבר את כל אשר אצוך ואהרון אחיך ידבר אל   11

[פרעה ושלח] את בני ישר[אל] ³[ו]אני אקשה את לב פרעה   12

[והרביתי את א]תתי [וא]ת מופתי בא[ר]ץ מצרים   13

Exodus 4Q22 (paleo Exod^m), Column 1

2   These are that Aaron and Moses to whom

3   the Lord said, Bring out the children of Israel from the land of Egypt according

4   to their armies. These are they which spake to Pharaoh king of Egypt to bring
    out the children of Israel

5   from Egypt: these are that Moses and Aaron. And it came to pass on the day
    when the Lord spake

6   unto Moses in the land of Egypt,

7   That the Lord spake unto Moses, saying, I am the Lord: speak thou unto
    Pharaoh king of Egypt

8   all that I say unto thee. And Moses said before the Lord,

9   Behold, I am of uncircumcised lips, and how shall Pharaoh hearken unto me?

10   And the Lord said unto Moses, See, I have made thee a god to Pharaoh: and
    Aaron thy brother shall be

11   thy prophet. Thou shalt speak all that I command thee: and Aaron thy brother
    shall speak unto

12   Pharaoh, that he send the children of Israel out of his land. And I will harden
    Pharaoh's heart,

13   and multiply my signs and my wonders in the land of Egypt.

(2)

PSALMS
תהילים

11Q5 (Psª)
18 x 71.5 cm • 30–50 CE

This impressive scroll is a liturgical collection of psalms and hymns, comprising parts of 41 biblical psalms (chiefly from chapters 101 to 50) in non-canonical sequence and with variations in detail. It also presents Apocryphal psalms (previously unknown hymns dealing with the future), as well as a prose passage about the psalms composed by King David: "… And the total was 4,050. All these he composed through prophecy, which was given him from before the Most High" (11QPsª 27:10–11).

The Psalms scroll, found in Cave 11 in 1956 and unrolled in 1961, is one of the longer texts from Qumran. Its surface is the thickest of any of the scrolls – it may be calfskin rather than sheepskin (the writing material most commonly used at Qumran). The writing is on the grain side. The scroll contains 28 incomplete columns of text, five of which are displayed here. It is clear that six to seven lines are missing from the bottom of each column. Column 22 bears the text of a non-canonical psalm (that is, not included in the Bible); known as "The Apostrophe to Zion", it is a hymn of praise for Jerusalem.

The scroll's script is of fine quality, with the letters carefully drawn in the Jewish bookhand style of the Herodian period. The Tetragrammaton (the four-lettered divine name) is inscribed in the palaeo-Hebrew script. On palaeographic grounds, the manuscript is dated between 30 and 50 CE.

Reference: Sanders, J.A., 1965, *Discoveries in the Judaean Desert*, vol. IV, Oxford.

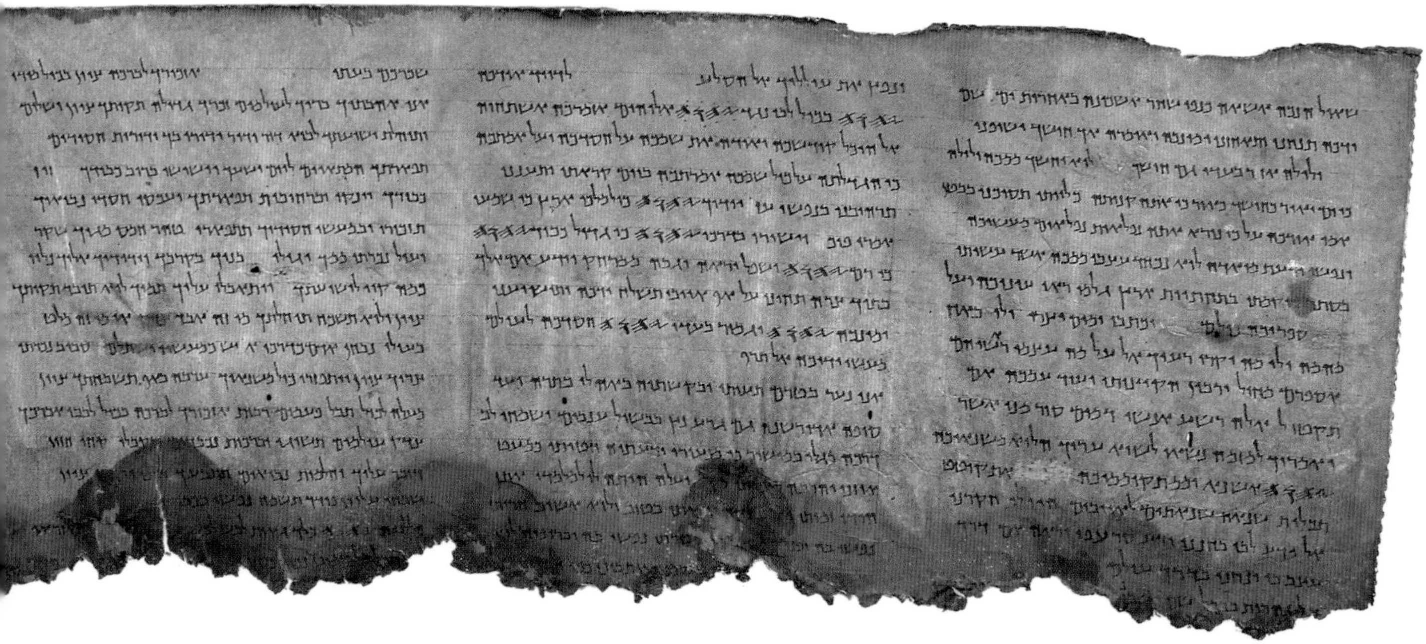

PSALMS

מזמור חיצוני

1 אזכורך לברכה ציון

בכול מודי אני אהבתיך

ברוך לעולמים זכרך

2 גדולה תקותך ציון

ושלום ותוחלת ישועתך לבוא

3 דור ודור ידורו בך

ודורות חסידים תפארתך

4 המתאוים ליום ישעך

וישישו ברוב כבודך

5 זיז כבודך יינקו

וברחובות תפארתך יעכסו

6 חסדי נביאיך תזכורי

ובמעשי חסידיך תתפארי

7 טהר חמס מגוך

שקר ועול נכרתו ממך

8 יגילו בניך בקרבך

וידידיך אליך נלוו

9 כמה קוו לישועתך

ויתאבלו עליך תמיד

10 לוא תובד תקותך ציון

ולוא תשכח תוחלתך

11 מי זה אבד צדק

או מי זה מלט בעולו

Psalms 11Q5 (Ps^a), Column 22, lines 1–11

1   I remember thee for blessing, O Zion;
    with all my might have I loved thee.
    May thy memory be blessed for ever!

2   Great is thy hope, O Zion;
    that peace and thy longed-for salvation will come.

3   Generation after generation will dwell in thee
    and generations of saints will be thy splendour:

4   those who yearn for the day of thy salvation
    that they may rejoice in the greatness of thy glory.

5   On (the) abundance of thy glory they are nourished
    and in thy splendid squares will they toddle.

6   The merits of thy prophets wilt thou remember,
    and in the deeds of thy pious ones wilt thou glory.

7   Purge violence from thy midst;
    falsehood and evil will be cut off from thee.

8   Thy sons will rejoice in thy midst
    and thy precious ones will be united with thee.

9   How they have hoped for thy salvation,
    thy pure ones have mourned for thee.

10 Hope for thee does not perish, O Zion,
    nor is hope in thee forgotten.

11 Who has ever perished (in) righteousness,
    or who has ever survived in his iniquity?

PSEUDO-EZEKIEL
פסבדו יחזקאל

4Q386
10 x 24 cm • Second century BCE

This manuscript is one of five copies of a previously unknown composition found at Qumran. This writing reworks the canonical prophesies of Ezekiel, including the Vision of the Dry Bones (Ezek. 37) and the Vision of the Chariot (Ezek. 1). Especially interesting is the version of the Vision of the Dry Bones. It is understood to represent resurrection at the End of Days as the reward of the righteous. This is, then, the earliest extant witness to such an interpretation.

The best preserved fragment of Pseudo-Ezekiel is the manuscript displayed here. It shows the upper sections of three consecutive columns. The second column deals with a non-biblical vision that was revealed to Ezekiel about future events in Egypt relating to the people of Israel. The events and figures involved are enigmatic, and the entire passage is open to more than one interpretation.

Reference: Dimant, D., *Discoveries in the Judaean Desert*, vol. XXX (in press), Oxford.

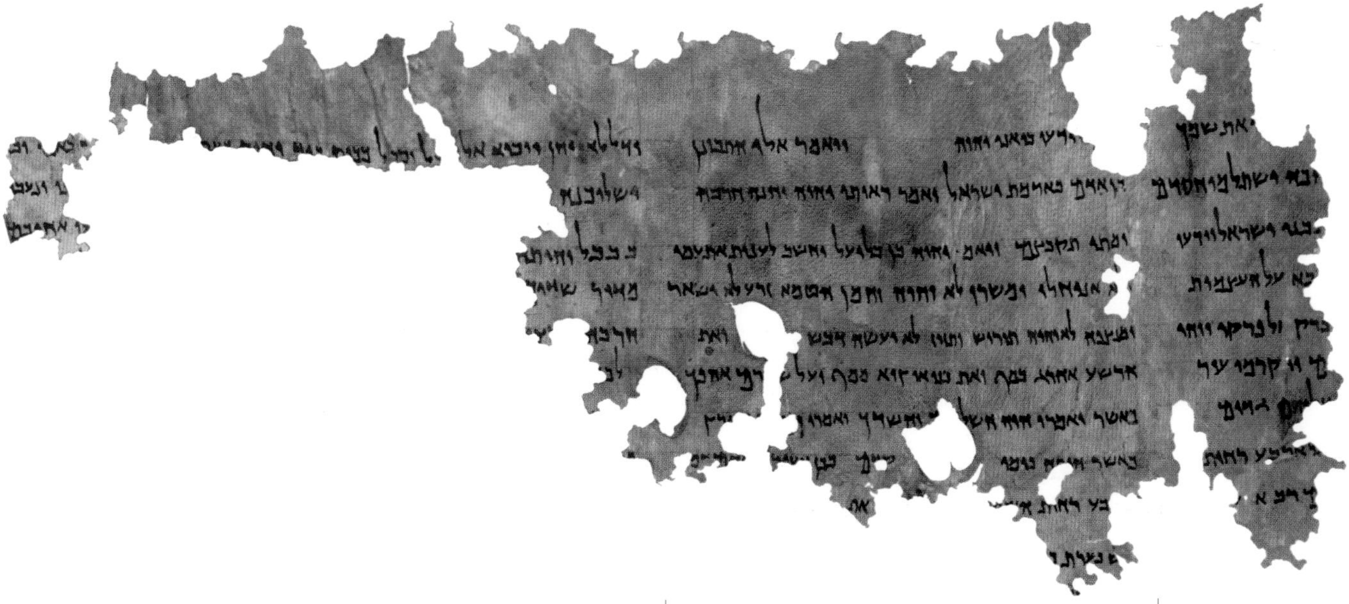

44

1 ‏[אר]ץ וידעו כי אני יהוה vac ויאמר אלי התבונן

2 ‏בן אדם באדמת ישראל ואמר ראיתי יהוה והנה חרבה

3 ‏ומתי תקבצם ויאמר יהוה בן בליעל יחשב לענות את עמי

4 ‏ולא אניח לו ומשרו לא יהיה והמן הטמא זרע לא ישאר

5 ‏ומנצפה לא יהיה תירוש ותזיז לא יעשה דבש v[ac] ואת

6 ‏רשע אהרג במף ואת בני אוציא ממף ועל ש[א]רם אהפך

Pseudo-Ezekiel 4Q386

1   [lan]d and they shall know that I am the Lord.' *vac* And he said to me, 'Look,

2   O son of man, at the land of Israel.' And I said, 'I have seen, Lord, and behold it lies waste,

3   and when will you gather them together?' And the Lord said, 'A son of Belial will scheme to oppress my people

4   but I will not allow him; and from his kin there will not be, nor will there be left from the impure one any seed;

5   and from the caperbush there shall be no wine, nor will a hornet make any honey. *v[a]c* And the

6   wicked one I will slay at Memphis but my children I will bring forth from Memphis, and their remnant I shall turn.[?]

NAHUM COMMENTARY
פשר נחום

4Q169
11 x 53 cm • Copied first century CE

The Nahum Commentary belongs to a literary genre which interprets the Scriptures with the intention of revealing allusions to current and future events. These events are related to the history of the sect, its leaders and its adversaries.

The biblical book of Nahum is a poem celebrating the destruction of Assyrian power in the fall of Nineveh. In this commentary, the sect interpreted the text in the light of the events of its own period. It is unusual, in that it mentions known historical figures, such as the Seleucid kings, Demetrius III and Antiochus IV, and the Hasmonean monarch, Alexander Jannaeus, who is called "the Lion of Wrath".

The commentary also mentions the tripartite division of Judaism of the time, referring to Ephraim (the Pharisees), Menasheh (the Sadducees) and Judah (the Essenes).

The commentary was composed in the second century BCE; the manuscript displayed here is a copy dating to the first century CE.

Reference: Allegro, J.M., 1968, *Discoveries in the Judaean Desert*, vol. V, Oxford.

48

1 [   ] מדור לרשעי גוים אשר הלך ארי לביא שם גור ארי

2 [ואין מחריד, פשרו על דמי]טריס מלך יון אשר בקש לבוא ירושלים בעצת דורשי החלקות

3 [ולא נתן אל את ירושלים] ביד מלכי יון מאנתיכוס עד עמוד מושלי כתיים ואחר תרמס

4 [   ] ארי טורף בדי גוריו מחנק ללביותיו טרף

5 [   ] פשרו] על כפיר החרון אשר יכה בגדוליו ואנשי עצתו

6 [ימלא טרף] חורה ומעונתו טרפה - פשרו על כפיר החרון

7 [אשר   ] משפט] מות בדורשי החלקות אשר יתלה אנשים חיים

1   Whither the lion, the lioness, the lion's cub

2   [and none to terrify, Its interpretation concerns Deme]trius King of Greece, who sought to enter Jerusalem by the counsel of the Seekers after Smooth Things

3   [and God did not surrender Jerusalem into] the hand of the Kings of Greece from Antiochus until the rise to power of rulers of the Kittim; but afterwards (the city) shall be trodden down.

4   [   ] The lion tears sufficient for his cubs and strangles prey for his lioness

5   [Its interpretation] concerns the Lion of Wrath who strikes by means of his great men, and the men of his counsel

6   [he filled with prey] his cave and his den with torn flesh. Its interpretation concerns the Lion of Wrath

7   [Who   sentence of] death on the Seekers after Smooth Things and who hangs men alive

5

COMMUNITY RULE
סרך היחד

4Q260
7.5 x 49 cm • Copied late first century BCE–early first century CE

50

Originally known as the Manual of Discipline, the Community Rule contains regulations ordering the life of the members of the *yaḥad*, the group within the Judaean Desert sect who chose to live communally. The rules of conduct, which are accompanied by admonitions and punishments to be imposed on violators, deal with the manner of joining the group, the relations between the members, their way of life and their beliefs. The sect divided humanity between the righteous and the wicked, and asserted that human nature and everything that happens in the world are irrevocably predestined. The scroll ends with songs of praise to God.

A complete copy of the scroll – 11 columns in length – was found in Cave 1, but 10 fragmentary copies were recovered in Cave 4 and a small section was found in Cave 5. The large number of manuscripts of this scroll, including the complete copy, attests to its importance for the sect.

This manuscript was copied between the late first century BCE and the early first century CE.

Reference: Alexander, P.S., and Vermes, G., 1998, *Discoveries in the Judaean Desert*, vol. XXVI, Oxford.

1 אר]חם   על כול סוררי דרך לוא אנחם בנכוחים עד תום

2 ד]רכ]ם ובליעל לוא אשמור בלבבי ולוא ישמע בפי

3 נבלות וכחש עוון [ומ]רמות וכזבים לוא ימצאו בשפתי

4 ופרי קודש בלשוני vac ושקוצים לוא ימצא

5 בה בהוד]ות אפ]ת[ח] vac פי]ו[צדקות אלתס]פר]

6 לשוני תמ]יד ומעל [אנשים ע]ד ת]ום פשעם] רקים]

7 [אשבית משפטי נדות ונפתלות] מ]דעת לבי בעצת תושיה]

1   [I will have no com]passion on any who deviate from the way. I will have no pity on the straightforward(?) till they have mended

2   their w[a]ys. And I will not keep Belial in my heart. And there shall not be heard in my mouth

3   foolish things and wicked lying, [and de]ceptions and falsehoods shall not be found on my lips.

4   And the fruit of holiness (shall be) on my tongue, *vac* and abominations shall not be found

5   thereon. In songs of thanksgi[ving I will o]pe[n] *vac* my mouth [and] my tongue shall rec[ount] the righteous acts of God

6   contin[uously, as well as the faithlessness] of men, un[til] their sinful rebellion [comes to an e]nd. [Vanities]

7   [I will cause to cease from my lips, impurities and perversions] from [the knowledge of my heart with wise counsel]

DAMASCUS DOCUMENT
ברית דמשק

4Q266 (D[f])
10 x 26.5 cm • Copied late first century BCE

Solomon Schechter's 1890 discovery of a copy of the Damascus Document (or Damascus Covenant) in the Cairo *genizah* may be regarded as the true starting point of modern scroll research. In his *Fragments of a Zadokite Work*, published in 1910, he presented two copies of a medieval text that he identified as being of a sectarian nature. Almost half a century passed before inscribed scrolls discovered in the Judaean Desert confirmed Schechter's identification and Second Temple period dating.

The Damascus Document includes two elements. The first is an admonition that implores the congregation to remain faithful to the covenant of those who retreated from Judaea to the "Land of Damascus". The second lists statutes dealing with vows and oaths, the tribunal, witnesses and judges, purification of water, Sabbath laws and ritual cleanliness. It calls for the abandonment of practices deemed contradictory to the sect's interpretation of the Torah.

Palaeographically, this fragment is the earliest of the eight fragments of the Damascus Document uncovered in Cave 4. The fragment exhibited is a late first century BCE copy.

Reference: Baumgarten, J.M., 1996, *Discoveries in the Judaean Desert*, vol. XVIII, Oxford.

1

2 ‏[מן העור   הכ]הן וראה הכהן אותו כמראי הבשר החי וכ[

3 ‏[   ] צרעת [ ] היאה האוחז {ת} ה בעור החי וכמשפט הזה [   ]

4 ‏[   ] וראה הכהן ביום השביעי והנא נוסף מן החי [אל]

5 ‏[המת   צ]רעת ממארת היא ומשפט נתק הרוש והז[קן]

6 ‏[   ] וראה הכהן וה[נ]א באה הרוח ברוש (ו)בזקן באוחז{ת}ה

7 ‏בגיד ופר[ח] הנגע מתחת הש[ע]ר והפך מרא[ת]ה לדק צוהב כי כעשב

8 ‏הוא אשר [י]ש הרחש תחתו vac ויקיץ שורשו ויבש פרחו ואשר

9 ‏אמר וצוה הכוהן וגלחו את ה{ב}ר{וש}ר} ואת הנתק לא יגלחו למען אשר

10 ‏י{ש}ספור הכוהן את השערות המיתות והחיות וראה אם יו{ש}סף מן

11 ‏כי החי אל המת בשבעת הימים טמא הואה ואם לו ליוסף מן הח[יות]

12 ‏על המיתות והגיד נמלא [ד]ם ור[ו]ח החיים עולה ויורדת בו [נרפא]

13 ‏הנגע זה משפט [תור]ת הצרעת לבני אהרון להבדיל ל[   ]

Damascus Document 4Q266 (D^f)

1

2   [than the skin   the pr]iest and the priest sees in it the appearance of living flesh [   ]

3   [it is *sara*^c*at*] which has taken hold of the living skin. A similar rule for [ ]

4   [   ] the priest shall see on the seventh day. If some of the living has been added

5   [to the dead   ] it is malignant [*sa*]*ra*^c*at*. And the rule *vac* for a scall of the head or the bea[rd]

6   [when the priest sees] that the spirit has entered the head or the beard, taking hold of

7   the blood vessels and [the malady has sprouted from beneath under the h]air, turning its appearance to fine yellowish; for it is like a plant

8   which has a worm under it *vac* which severs its root and makes its blossom wither. And as to that

9   which he said, 'And the priest shall order that they shave the head, but not the scall', (this is) in order that

10   the priest may count the dead and live hair and see whether any has been added from

11   the live to the dead during the seven days, (in which case) he is unclean; while if none has been added from the li[ve]

12   to the dead, and the blood vessel is filled with bl[ood] and the sp[ir]it of life pulsates up and down in it

13   the malady [is healed.] This is the rule of the [la]w of *sara*^c*at* for the sons of Aaron to separate [ ]

SOME TORAH PRECEPTS
מקצת מעשה התורה

4Q394 (MMT)
16.5 x 17 cm • Copied late first century BCE–early first century CE

This scroll is a sectarian polemical document, of which six incomplete manuscripts have been discovered. Together, these fragments provide a composite text of about 130 lines, covering probably two-thirds of the original. The initial part of the text is completely missing.

The document, apparently in letter form, is unique in language, style and content. It probably consisted of four sections: the opening formula, now lost; a calendar of 364 days; a list of more than 20 rulings in religious law (*halakhot*), most of which are peculiar to the sect; and an epilogue that deals with the separation of the sect from the multitude of the people and attempts to persuade the addressee to adopt the sect's legal views. These *halakhot* deal chiefly with the Temple and its ritual. The author states that disagreement on these matters caused the sect to secede from Israel.

As the beginning of the text has been lost, the identities of both the author and the addressee are unknown. However, a commentary (*pesher*) to Psalm 37 relates that the "Teacher of Righteousness" conveyed a letter to his opponent, the "Wicked Priest". This may well be a reference to this document, which is addressed to "the leader of Israel".

In general, the script belongs to the semi-formal tradition of Herodian times. This manuscript was copied at some time between the late first century BCE and the early first century CE.

Most of the manuscripts are inscribed on parchment, although several papyrus fragments also have survived.

Reference: Qimron, E., and Strugnell, J., 1994, *Discoveries in the Judaean Desert*, vol. X, Oxford.

SOME TORAH PRECEPTS

52 [וא]ף על החרשים שלוא שמעו חוק [ומ]שפט וטהרה ולא

53 [ש]מעו משפטי ישראל כי שלוא ראה ולוא שמע לוא

54 [י]דע לעשות והמה באים לטה[ר]ת המקדש

55 [ו]אף על המוצקות אנחנו אומר[ים] שהם שאין בהם

56 [ט]הרה ואף המוצקות אינם מבדילות בין הטמא

57 [ל]טהור כי לחת המוצקות והמקבל מהמה כהם

58 לחה אחת ואין להבי למחני הק[ו]דש כלבים שהם

59 אוכלים מקצת [ע]צמות המק[דש ו]הבשר עליהם כי

60 ירושלים היאה מחנה הקדש והיא המקום

61 שבחר בו מכל שבטי י[שראל כי יר]ושלים היא ראש

62 [מ]חנות ישראל ואף ע[ל מ]טעת עצ[י] המאכל הנטע

52   and concerning the deaf who have not heard the laws and the judgments and the purity regulations, and have not

53   heard the ordinances of Israel, since he who has not seen or heard

54   does not know how to obey (the Law): nevertheless they have access to the sacred food.

55   And concerning liquid streams: we are of the opinion that they are not

56   pure, and that these streams do not act as a separative between impure

57   and pure (liquids). For the liquid of streams and (that) of (the vessel) which receives them are alike, (being)

58   a single liquid. And one must not let dogs enter the holy camp, since they

59   may eat some of the bones of the sanctuary while the flesh is (still) on them. For

60   Jerusalem is the camp of holiness, and is the place

61   which He has chosen from among all the tribes of Israel. For Jerusalem is the capital of the

62   camps of Israel. And concerning (the fruits of) the trees for food planted

THANKSGIVING PSALMS
הודיות

4Q427 (4QH[a])
16 x 17.5 cm • Copied 75 BCE–end of the first century BCE

The Thanksgiving Psalms (*Hodayot*) comprise a collection of about 30 poetic compositions. Modelled to some extent on the form of the biblical psalms of "individual thanksgiving", they express gratitude and praise for what God has done for the psalmist, especially in granting knowledge and insight, deliverance from distress, and membership in the community. In many of the psalms, a formulaic introduction has been preserved: "I thank you, O Lord, because …"; there is no set conclusion. In some psalms, there is a stronger sense of the individual speaking as one specially chosen to have a distinct role in instructing others; many scholars have suggested that these psalms were composed by the "Teacher of Righteousness". Other psalms have more focus on the community and contain extended reflections on human weakness and sinfulness and the greatness of divine grace and mercy.

There are eight copies of the *Hodayot*, arranged in different collections and orders. The best preserved manuscript – from Cave 1 at Qumran – was published by E. Sukenik in 1954 (1QH[a]). The six manuscripts from Cave 4, published in 1999, are more fragmentary. In the fragments from the Cave 4 manuscript displayed here, the psalms are arranged in a different order from 1QH[a].

This copy of the *Hodayot* is written in a Hasmonean or early-Herodian semi-cursive hand and has been dated from 75 BCE to the end of the century.

Reference: Schuller, E., 1999, *Discoveries in the Judaean Desert*, vol. XXIX, Oxford.

THANKSGIVING PSALMS

זמרו ידידים שירו למלכ 13

[הכבוד שמחו בע]דת אל הרנינו באהלי ישועה הללו במעון 14

[קודש ר]וממו יחד בצבא עולם הבו גדול לאלנו וכבוד למלכנו 15

[הקדי]שו שמו בשפתי עוז ולשון נצח הרימו לבד קולכמה 16

[בכ]ול קצים השמיעו הגידנה הביעו בשמחות עולמים ואין 17

[ה]שבת השחוו ביחד קהל ברכו המפלי גאות ומודיע עוז ידו 18

13   … Sing praise, O beloved ones, sing to the King of

14   [glory, rejoice in the congre]gation of God, ring out joy in the tents of
salvation, give praise in the [holy] habitation,

15   [ex]tol together among the eternal hosts, ascribe greatness to our God and
glory to our king.

16   [Sanc]tify his name with strong lips and mighty tongue, raise up together
your voice

17   [at a]ll times, sound aloud joyful music, rejoice with everlasting joy

18   [un]ceasingly, worship in the common assembly. Bless the one who
wonderfully does majestic deeds, and makes known his strong hand,

9

WAR RULE
סרך המלחמה

11Q14
14.5 x 16 cm • Copied c. 20–50 CE

This fragment is part of a composition that describes the end of an eschatological war in which the leader of the evil *Kittim* (the Romans) was killed. It also tells of how the land was cleansed of contaminant enemy corpses and repentance from sin took place. The fragment on display is from the end of the text and contains a benediction, bestowing blessings on the eschatological community of Israel – probably the outcome of cleansing and repentance.

This fragment overlaps with a text recovered from Cave 4 that has been dubbed the "Pierced Messiah Text" (4Q285). Both of these fragments may well represent versions of the missing finale of the War Scroll from Cave 1, in which it is said that the forces of good and evil will clash on the battlefield "at the end of days". A major difference between the two lies in the identification of the central figure: 4Q285 deals with the "Prince of the Congregation" and the War Rule highlights the figure of the high priest.

The handwriting is the developed Herodian formal script of c. 20–50 CE.

Reference: García-Martínez, F., et al, 1998, *Discoveries in the Judaean Desert*, vol. XXIII, Oxford.

ברכם ב
שראל ברכנם
ובהמה יענו קורא
אלו וברכנם כול
בלאבא קורישו

וברך אתכם אל עולמי ויאר פנו אלוכם ופתחו לכם את
אוצרו הטוב אשר בשמאם להורגר על ארצכם
אשר עבטו טלו ו טור מרוח ובלקוש ביעתו ולתת לכם פרי
רבות ודגן תרירוש ויצהר לרוב והארץ תנבב לכם פר
תעגם ואכלתנו והרישנתם ואנו בשבלוה בארצכם
לא מויילד שיען ורירזון לא אראה בתבא תבתח
שול בשותבם ומאד רעה שבטנך כל
ר בארצבם בא אל עבנך ובאבו
בעזתבם ושם קורישו קורא עלובם

WAR RULE

7   יברך אתכם אל עליון ויאר פניו אליכם ויפתח לכם את

8   אוצרו הטוב אשר בשמים להוריד על ארצכמה

9   גשמי ברכה טל ומטר יורה ומלקוש בעתו ולתת לכם פר[י]

10   תנובות דגן תירוש ויצהר לרוב והארץ תנובב לכם פרי

11   [ע]דנים ואכלתם והדשנתם vac ואין משכלה בארצכם

7   God Most High will bless you and shine his face upon you, and he will open for you

8   his rich storehouse in the heavens, to send down upon your land

9   showers of blessing, dew and rain, the early rain and the latter rain in its season, and to give you frui[t],

10   produce, grain, wine and oil in abundance; and the land will produce for you [d]elightful fruit

11   so that you will eat and grow fat. *vac* And none will miscarry in your land,

CALENDRICAL DOCUMENT
משמרות

4Q325
6 x 10.6 cm • End of the first century BCE

Fragments of some 20 calendar-related compositions of various types were discovered at Qumran, mostly in Cave 4. The manuscript presented here illustrates the Covenanters' method of synchronising the holy seasons – festivals, Sabbaths and the "first days of the month" – with the two annual one-week terms of service in the Temple of the priestly courses (*Mishmarot*) in a six-year cycle. The rotating system facilitated the adjustment of the biblical roster of 24 courses (Chron. 24:7–9) that served in the lunar year of 354 days to the Covenanters' solar calendar of 364 days (that is, 52 weeks), by having three courses serve for a third week each and two for an additional half-week.

Proper chronology was fundamental to the Covenanters' messianic–millenarian expectations which derived from and depended on an accurately defined succession of periods in history. The correct execution of the priestly services, rivetted to the progression of the holy seasons, played a vital role in this time system.

This composition originally enumerated the annual holy seasons over a period of six years, together with the names of the priestly courses that officiated on each of these days. Partly preserved are references to festivals known from biblical sources – the "Sacrifice of the Passover Lamb" and the "Waving of the First Sheaf" – and to "the first of the (second, third and sixth) month", as well as to the Covenanters' special festivals of the "First Wine (Grapes)", the "First Oil (Olives)" and the "Offering of the Wood (for the altar)", which are not explicitly recorded in the Bible.

References: Talmon, S., 1995, "A Calendrical Document from Qumran Cave 4 (*Mishmarot* D, 4Q325)", in *Solving Riddles and Untying Knots*, Indiana, pp. 327–344. Talmon, S., *Discoveries in the Judaean Desert*, vol. XXI (forthcoming), Clarendon Press, Oxford.

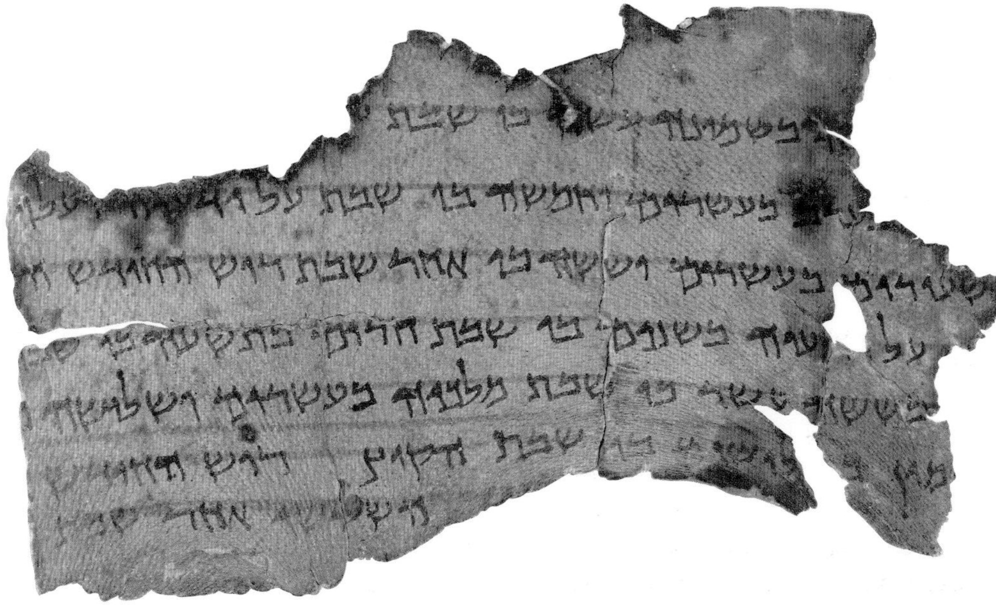

1   [הפסח יום שלי]שי בשמונה עשר בו שבת ע[ל יו]יריב

2   [בערב בעשרים וחמשה בו שבת על ידעיה ועלו]   [   ]

3   [מוע]ד שעורים בעשרים וששה בו אחר שבת רוש החודש ה[ש]ני

4   [בששה בשבת] על ידעיה בשנים בו שבת חרים בתשעה בו שבת

5   [שעורים] בששה עשר בו שבת מלכיה בעשרים ושלושה ב[ו

6   [שבת מי]מין בשלושים בו שבת הקוץ vac רוש החודש

7   השלישי אחר שבת   [v]a[c   ]

1   [… the Passah on the thi]rd [day] (of the week); on the eighteenth in it (the first month) Sabbath (on which) ent[ers Jehojarib

2   ]in the evening. On the twenty-fifth in it Sabbath (on which) enters Jedaᶜjah and enter[

3   the festival of] the (First) Grain (falls) on the twenty-six in it after the Sabbath; the beginning of the second mon[th

4   (falls) on the sixth (day) (of the week in which)] entered Jedaᶜjah; on the second in it Sabbath Harim. On the ninth in it Sabbath

5   Seᶜorim]; on the sixteenth in it Sabbath Malkiah. On the twenty-third in [it

6   Sabbath Mi]jamin. On the thirtieth in it Sabbath Hakkos *vac* the beginning of the third

7   *vac* month after Sabbath

ENOCH
חנוך

4Q212 (En ar⁹)
11.5 x 28 cm • Copied 50–1 BCE

One of the most important Apocryphal works of the Second Temple period is Enoch. According to the biblical narrative (Gen. 5:21–24), Enoch lived for 365 years and "walked with God; then he was no more for God took him".

Rabbinic sources and pseudepigraphic literature attach many tales and legends to this figure. He is all-wise, knowing the secrets of the universe and is the source of information for natural and supernatural occurrences. The fullest portrait of Enoch emerges in 1 Enoch, a work preserved in its entirety only in Ge'ez (Old Ethiopic).

The Book of Enoch is the earliest of the pseudepigraphic books. It is quoted in the Book of Jubilees and in the Testaments of the Twelve Patriarchs and is referred to in the New Testament (Jude 1:14).

In all likelihood, the original language of most of this work was Aramaic, which was lost in antiquity. Portions of a Greek translation were discovered in Egypt, and quotations were known from the church fathers. The discovery of the texts from Cave 4 has finally provided us with parts of the Aramaic original, covering 1 Enoch. The text presented here is from the composition known as the Apocalypse of Weeks – the eighth week, in which "there shall be built the Royal Temple of the Great One … for all generations for ever".

The Qumran manuscripts of Enoch have been dated palaeographically to some time between the early second century and the end of the first century BCE. This manuscript is a copy dated to 50–1 BCE.

Reference: Milik, J.T., 1976, "The Books of Enoch: Aramaic Fragments of Qumran Cave 4", Oxford University Press, Oxford.

ENOCH

15 ומן בתרה יקום שבוע תמיני ‹ד› קשוט דבה תתיה[ב חרב]

16 לכול קשיטין למעבד דין קשוט מן כול רשיעין

17 ויתיהבון בידהון ועם סופה יקנון נכסין בקשוט

18 ויתבנא היכל [מ[ל]כ]ות רבא ברבות זוה לכול דרי עלמין

15 And thereafter shall arise the eighth week, that of righteousness, in which [a sword] shall be given

16 to all the righteous, to exact a righteous judgment from all the wicked,

17 and they shall be delivered into their hands. And with its end they shall acquire riches in righteousness,

18 and there shall be built the royal Temple of the Great One in His glorious splendour, for all generations for ever.

12

PHYLACTERY
תפילין

4Q138, 4Q136, 4Q134, 4Q143 (Phyl K, I, G, P)
1.8 x 5.5/4.2 cm • Copied first century CE

Qumran has provided us with the earliest remains of phylacteries (or *tefillin*), both the leather containers and inscribed strips of parchment. The command, "And thou shalt bind them for a sign upon thy hand, and they shall be for frontlets between thine eyes" (Deut. 6:8) was practised by Jews from early times. In the Second Temple period, the sages established that phylacteries would include four scriptural passages (Exod. 13:1–10 and 13:11–16 and Deut. 6:4–9, 11:13–21) serving "as a sign and a reminder".

The phylacteries were inscribed in clear minuscule characters on tiny strips of parchment which were folded over to fit into the minute compartments stamped into leather containers. Phylacteries were worn on the left arm and on the forehead, a custom practised by Jews to this day.

Some of the phylacteries found at Qumran deviate from the traditional passages prescribed by the sages. This variation, as well as other irregularites noted by scholars who have been studying the texts, led to the conclusion that at least some of the phylacteries are sectarian.

Phyl K bears the text of Deut. 10:12–11:7 (obverse) and Deut. 11:7–12 (reverse), neither complying with the passages prescribed by the sages.

Phyl K is a copy dated to the first century CE.

Reference: de Vaux, R., and Milik, J.T., 1977, *Discoveries in the Judaean Desert*, vol. IV, Oxford, pp. 80–85.

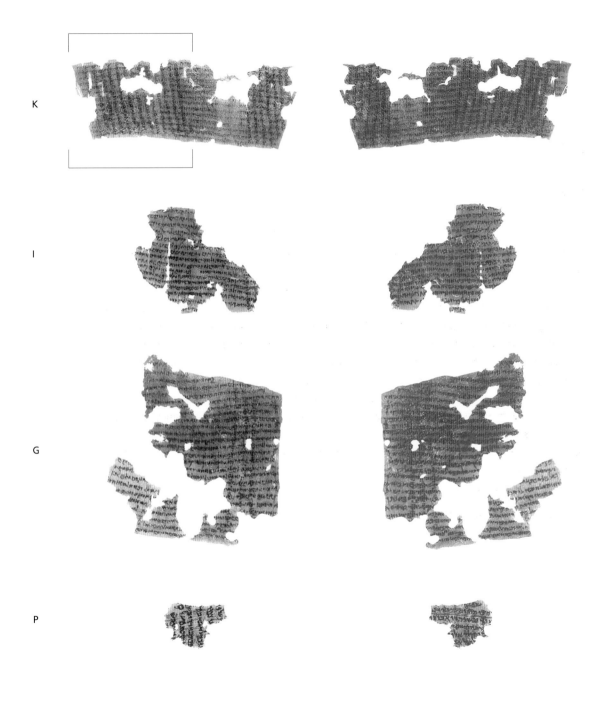

K

I

G

P

REVERSE

PHYLACTERY

עיניכמה ....

15 הראות את כו[ל] מ[עשי י] הוה הגדול

16 אשר עשה אתכמה ושמרת ה

17 את כול המצוה אשר אנ( )וכי מצ

18 וכה היום למען תחזקו ועברתמה

19 ובתמה וירשתמה את הארץ אש

20 אתמה ע[וברי]ם את הירדן שמה

21 לרשת [ה ול]מען תארכון ימים על

22 האדמ[ה א]שר נשבע יהוה לאבו

23 תכמה [לתת לה]מה ולזרעמה אחרי

24 [המ]ה ארץ [זב]ת חלב ודבש כי הארץ

25 אשר אתמה באים שמה לרשתה לוא

26 כארץ מצרים היאה אשר יצאתה מ

27 שמה אשר תזרע את זרעכה והשק

[ב]רג[ל]ליכה]

for your eyes

15   have seen all the great work of the Lord

16   which he did. You shall therefore keep

17   all the commandment which I command

18   you this day, that you may be strong, and go in

19   and take possession of the land

20   which you are going over [the Jordan]

21   to possess, and that you may live long in

22   the land which the Lord swore to your fathers

23   to give to them and to their descendants,

24   a land flowing with milk and honey. For the land

25   which you are entering to take possession of it

26   is not like the land of Egypt, from which you have come,

27   where you sowed your seed and watered it with your feet,

FROM THE QUMRAN RUIN

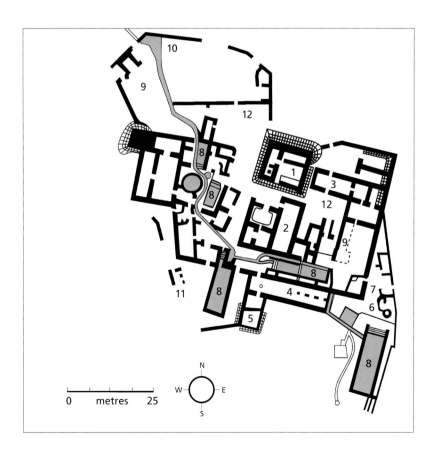

1 Tower
2 Scriptorium
3 Kitchen
4 Refectory
5 Larder
6 Kiln
7 Pottery workshop
8 Cisterns, ritual baths
9 Former ritual baths
10 Aqueduct
11 Stables
12 Courtyards

water system

N
W — E
S

0   metres   25

STONE VESSELS

Stone vessels, usually made of easily workable soft limestone, were common in the Jerusalem area in the late Second Temple period. Stone vessels of expert workmanship and a variety of shapes and sizes were found in abundance in Qumran.

It is evident that the use of stone vessels was extensive. The reason for their existence can be found in Jewish ritual law (*halakhah*). Stone – as opposed to pottery – does not become ritually unclean. Jewish law maintains that pottery vessels that have become ritually unclean must be broken, never to be used again, whereas in similar circumstances stone vessels retain their ritual purity and need not be discarded.

Some of these vessels served the same functions as ceramic vessels, and some had particular shapes and functions. Although the raw material is common in Jerusalem, the cost of production was, no doubt, far greater than that of pottery. The widespread manufacture of stone vessels came to an end with the destruction of the Second Temple (70 CE).

LARGE GOBLET
Limestone
height: 72 cm

This vessel was produced on a
lathe, probably in Jerusalem, and
shows excellent craftsmanship.
It is surprising that an ancient lathe
was capable of supporting and
working such a large and heavy
stone block.

MEASURING CUP
Limestone
height: 13 cm

Cylindrical cups of this type, ranging
in height between 5 cm and 15 cm,
are frequently found in sites of the
Second Temple period. It is believed
that their capacities correspond to
the dry and liquid measures
mentioned in the Mishnah.
   This vessel type was pared with
a knife or chisel, and its surface
was left unsmoothed. The vertical
handles rule out the possibility that
it might have been produced on a
rotating lathe.

POTTERY

Pottery, coins and written material found at an archaeological site allow for the establishment of a relative and an absolute chronological and cultural framework. Consequently, the pottery found in the Dead Sea area disclosed many facets of the Qumran story.

The vessels shown here are representative of the finds from the immediate area of Qumran. Items from the surrounding caves and openings in the cliffs proved to be identical to those excavated at the Qumran site itself. It seems to have been a regional centre – most likely, a single pottery workshop supplied the entire area.

Despite the large quantity of ceramic vessels found at Qumran, the repertoire is limited – apart from a large number of cylindrical scroll jars, it consists chiefly of modest items of daily use, such as juglets, flasks, drinking cups, cooking pots, serving dishes and bowls. A storeroom found during the excavation contained more than a thousand pottery items arranged by usage: vessels for cooking, serving, pouring, drinking and dining.

References: de Vaux, R., 1973, *Archaeology and the Dead Sea Scrolls*, Oxford University Press, Oxford. Lapp, P., 1961, *Palestinian Ceramic Chronology, 200 BC–AD 70*, New Haven.

JARS WITH LIDS
Pottery
height: 40–50 cm

Some of the Dead Sea Scrolls were found in cylindrical pottery jars of this type, which are unknown elsewhere. The discovery of these singular vessels in the Qumran excavations as well as in the caves is considered by many to be convincing evidence of the link between the settlement and the caves. These jars, as well as the other pottery vessels recovered at Qumran, are probably of local manufacture.

INKWELL
Pottery
height: 5 cm
diameter: 5 cm

Two inkwells – one of pottery and another of bronze – were found at the Qumran excavations among the debris of a collapsed upper storey. After careful reassemblage, the debris proved to contain the remains of a low, smoothly plastered mudbrick table (about five metres long), two shorter tables and a bench, suggesting to the site's excavators scribal activity in a scriptorium. It is feasible that many of the manuscripts were written or copied locally, although manuscripts of earlier date and other locations may still be found.

The cylindrical pottery vessel above, missing the loop handle, has a flat base and a small, circular opening with a rim. This type of vessel also has been found in excavations in Jerusalem.

PLATES, BOWLS AND GOBLETS
Pottery
diameter: 13.6–16.4 cm

Piles of plates, bowls and goblets
were found in one of the rooms at
Qumran. This room probably was
a pantry. It was located near the
assembly room, which may have
served as a dining room.

The wheel-made plates are
shallow, with a ring base and
upright rim. The firing is metallic.
Hundreds of plates were recovered,
most of them complete. Some bore
traces of soot.

DRIED DATES AND PITS

Food remains often are found in
desert sites. They provide us with
some insight into ancient diets.
The most common food remains
are date pits, olive stones and the
shells of pomegranates and nuts.

JUGS AND JUGLETS
Pottery

COOKING POTS, BOWL AND FUNNEL
Pottery

WOODEN ARTEFACTS

Wooden artefacts are rare finds in the material culture of the ancient Near East, and few specimens from the Roman period have survived. The considerable quantity of organic finds coming from the Judaean Desert is an exceptional occurrence, a result of the arid climatic conditions prevailing in the area. The finds include many wooden objects – bowls, boxes, mirror frames and handles, combs and spinning equipment – all contributing to the study of ancient woodworking techniques.

COMBS
Boxwood
height: 5–6.1 cm
width: 6 cm

Similar to most of the ancient
combs, these boxwood combs are
two-sided. One side has closely
spaced teeth for straightening the
hair. The other side provides more
teeth – for delousing.

BOWL
Wood
diameter: 11 cm
height: 4.9 cm

This deep bowl with flat ring base
was expertly turned on a lathe.
A ridge at the bottom creates a
groove in the interior. The upright
band-like rim has incisions at the
top, on both the interior and
exterior surfaces.

BOWL
Wood
diameter: about 13.5 cm
(part of the bowl is missing)
height: 6 cm

This deep bowl was turned on
a lathe. It has a flat ring base
and a thickened rim. Three sets
of double concentric incisions
decorate the exterior.

BASKETRY AND CORDAGE

Basketry and cordage represent a major type of perishable material retrieved in the arid part of Israel. The basketry fragments on display are made of date palm leaves, a material convenient for making baskets and mats. The technique used is a type of plaiting that was popular during Roman times and remained in favour through the following centuries; a variant is still used in the Near East today.

Because of the exceptional conditions inside caves in the Dead Sea region, several baskets and mats of plaited weave survived intact. Their survival permitted the reconstruction of the Qumran plaited basket, made of a single plait composed of several elements and spiralling from base to rim. The coiled plait was not sewn together; instead, successive courses were joined around cords as the weaving progressed. In a complete basket, the cords are not visible, but they form horizontal ridges and a ribbed texture. Each basket has two arched handles made from palm-fibre rope. Much ingenuity is displayed by the way in which they were attached to the rims by passing reinforcing cords through the plaited part of the basket.

Basketware was probably very common, as it is today, in household activities. However, in times of need, baskets and mats also served for collecting and wrapping the bones and skulls of the dead.

The medium-thick ropes on display may have been used in packing and tying bundles and waterskins. The compound cables made of plied cords possibly served as handles.

Tamar Schick

BASKET FRAGMENTS
Palm leaves
length: 13–14 cm
width: 21–23.5 cm

ROPES AND CABLES
Palm leaves, palm fibres and
undetermined rushes
diameter: 6–16 mm

LEATHER OBJECTS

The Judaean Desert has yielded a fair number of leather objects, permitting study of ancient tanning techniques. Waterskins, large bags, pouches, purses, sandals and garments have been found in varied desert sites.

The majority of leather objects are of sheepskin. A few pieces, particularly those used as patches, are of goat- and calfskin. The skins were vegetable-tanned, mostly with gall and pomegranates.

Exhibited here are sandal soles of the *solea* type, found in the Qumran area. These soles are made of two layers of leather secured with leather bindings. Tabs entered the upper sole, through slits situated near the heel. The upper part of each tab (non-existent in the sandals on display) usually was pierced by two vertical slits, through which the main strap was threaded. The two ends of the main strap were then threaded into a slit near the toe, where they were tied, holding the foot onto the sole. Decorative intersecting incisions on the upper soles also may have had a practical purpose.

SANDALS
Leather
length: 23.5–24 cm

A

B

PHYLACTERY CASES
Leather

Phylacteries, or *tefillin*, are small, square boxes worn on the left arm and forehead. They serve as a sign and a reminder that the Lord brought the children of Israel out of Egypt (Exod. 13:9, 16). The command, "And thou shall bind them for a sign upon thy hand, and they shall be as frontlets between thine eyes" (Deut. 6:8), was practised by Jews from early times.

In the Second Temple period, the sages established that phylacteries would include four scriptural passages inscribed on parchment placed in a box-like container. Qumran has provided us with the earliest remains of the leather containers and the inscribed parchments.

TYPE A
dimensions: 1 x 2–3 cm

This phylactery case has two parts stitched together. It is a four-compartment case, to be worn on the head. Each compartment held a minute roll.

TYPE B
dimensions: 2.2 x 1.2 cm

Worn on the arm, this case has only one compartment. It is formed of a single piece of leather folded in two, with one half deeply stamped out to form a cavity to hold a minute roll. A fine leather thong was inserted at the middle, and the halves were folded over and stitched together.

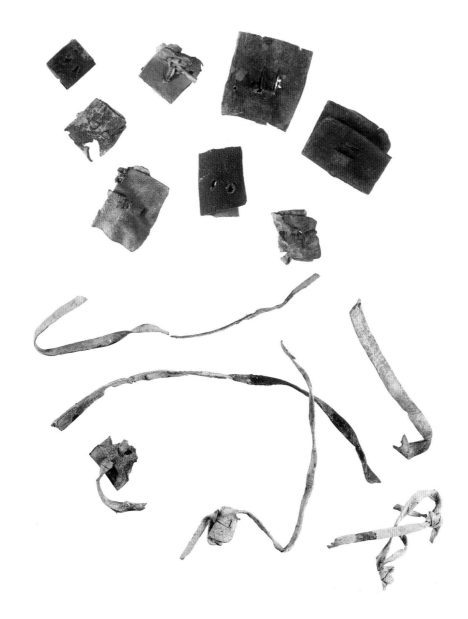

LEATHER SCROLL FASTENERS

TABS
length: 1.7–2.7 cm
width: 1.4–3.3 cm

THONGS
length: 7–30 cm
width: 0.3–0.8 cm

The tabs and thongs shown above probably were used to bind and secure individual scrolls (see replica at left). The fastening is thought to consist of a slotted tab folded over the edge of the scroll with a thong inserted through its slot. The thong could be tightened and then wound around the scroll. The fasteners, generally made of leather, were prepared in different sizes. The leather thongs also may have been used in the making of phylacteries.

TEXTILES AND SPINNING EQUIPMENT

The textile on display is one of many pieces found in 1949 in some of the Qumran caves. The pieces appear to have come from small cloths, ranging in size from 57 x 60 cm to 27 x 23 cm. They usually have one or two cut edges, hinting that the original loom-woven cloth was larger and wider. The cut edges were rolled and whipped. The yarn is S-spun, the proper way to spin flax, with consideration for the natural twist of the fibres. The linen is usually of fair quality in an even linen weave. The majority of the cloths are plain, although some have a fringe, with or without an open space at the end of the cloth. Several cloths have a corded starting border, indicating a somewhat primitive loom, possibly the warp-weighted loom or the two-beamed vertical loom. The only form of coloured decoration, although rare, is thin bands, usually two weft lines each, of indigo-dyed linen threads. Sometimes, as in the piece on display, the rolled edge is oversewn with a blue thread.

It seems probable that all the cloths from Qumran are associated in one way or another with the scrolls. Some of them certainly were scroll wrappers; the remains of one scroll were found wrapped in a small square of linen. Other cloths, found folded into pads, may have formed packing for worn-out scrolls inside the jars. Still other pieces – with corners twisted or tied around with linen cord – were probably protective covers, tied over the jars' tops. A few deteriorated textiles show repairs and patching (see the textile on display).

Materials related to spinning – spindles, shafts and whorls – have also been found. Spinning involves both drawing out the fibres of the raw material and twisting them into thread. The spindle usually consists of a stick or a shaft and a flywheel or spindle-whorl of some weight, giving momentum. Shafts, which were usually made of wood, have rarely survived; whorls, of such durable materials as stone, clay, bone, ivory and glass, are more common finds in excavations.

Tamar Schick

Reference: Crowfoot, G.M., 1955, *Discoveries in the Judaean Desert*, vol. I, Oxford, pp. 18–38.

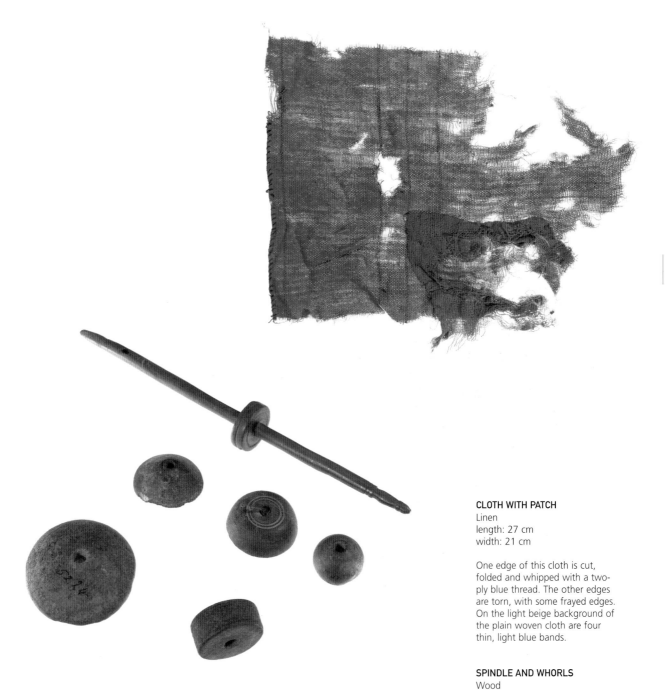

CLOTH WITH PATCH
Linen
length: 27 cm
width: 21 cm

One edge of this cloth is cut,
folded and whipped with a two-
ply blue thread. The other edges
are torn, with some frayed edges.
On the light beige background of
the plain woven cloth are four
thin, light blue bands.

SPINDLE AND WHORLS
Wood
length of shaft: 23.5 cm
diameter of shaft: 0.9 cm
height of whorl: 0.9 cm
diameters of whorls: 0.5–1 cm

HOARD OF COINS

In the 1955 season of excavations at Qumran, three intact ceramic vessels containing 561 silver coins were found under a doorway. The vessels were filled to the brim with coins, and the mouth of one of the vessels was covered with a palm-fibre stopper.

Père Roland de Vaux, excavator of Qumran, relied heavily on the coin evidence for his dating and interpretations of the various phases of the site. The early coins in the hoard were Seleucid *tetradrachms* of the third quarter of the second century BCE, minted in Tyre, as well as six Roman Republican coins from the middle of the first century BCE. The bulk of the hoard represents the autonomous continuation of the Seleucid mint: the well-known series of Tyrian *shekalim* and half-*shekalim*, minted from 126/125 BCE onwards. These are the same coins that were prescribed in the Temple for the poll tax and other payments. The latest coins in the hoard date to 9/8 BCE.

Two of the three hoard vessels are of a type otherwise unknown in the ceramic repertoire at Qumran. De Vaux suggested that the hoard corroborated the information in the Community Rule, which relates that new adherents in the sect were to surrender their worldly goods to the treasurer of the community. The vessels' contents would then constitute the deposit of one or a number of new adherents. A second possibility is that the hoard was the collection of half-*shekalim* towards some future payment of a Temple tax.

Exhibited here are 18 *shekalim*, half-*shekalim* and *denars* minted between 133 and 10/9 BCE.

Donald T. Ariel

References: de Vaux, R., 1973, *Archaeology and the Dead Sea Scrolls*, Oxford University Press, Oxford; Magness, J., 1998, "Two Notes on the Archaeology of Qumran", in *Bulletin of the American Schools of Oriental Research 312*, pp. 37–44.

HOARD OF COINS
Silver
diameter 1.9–2.8 cm

Shekalim and half-*shekalim*, part
of a hoard of 561 coins found in
vessels under a doorway at Qumran.

GLOSSARY

The publisher gratefully acknowledges *The Macquarie Dictionary* (3rd edn, 1997, Macquarie Library) for the definitions of foreign or unfamiliar words and terms used in this glossary.

Aaron The first high priest of the Hebrews and the brother of Moses (see Exodus 4:14).

Alexander the Great 356–323 BCE, king of Macedonia 336–323 BCE; conqueror of Greek city-states and Persian Empire from Asia Minor and Egypt to India.

Antioch A town in southern Turkey, capital of the ancient kingdom of Syria 300-64 BCE.

Antiochus III ("the Great") 242–187 BCE, king of Syria 223–187 BCE; extended Seleucid empire; fought against the Romans by whom he was defeated in Greece (191 BCE) and Asia Minor (190 BCE).

Antiochus IV Died 164? BCE; king of Syria 175–164? BCE; provoked the revolt of the Maccabees (167 BCE) by attacking the Jews.

apocalyptic Pertaining to a genre of literature that divulges otherworldly secrets about the nature of God and the heavens and the End of Days. Also used to describe the immediate messianism that is often part of these texts.

Apocrypha Technically, the books found in the Septuagint Greek Bible but not in the canon of the Hebrew Bible. More loosely, the term refers to pseudobiblical books composed in the Second Temple period.

Aramaic Any group of Semitic languages which became the speech of Syria, Palestine and Mesopotamia after c. 300 BCE, including Syriac and the language of Christ, in which many important Jewish texts were composed.

Asia Minor In ancient usage, a vast plateau between the Black Sea and the Mediterranean.

Assyria An ancient empire in south-west Asia; greater extent about 750–612 BCE from Egypt to the Tigris River and Persian Gulf.

Bactria An ancient country in western Asia between the Oxus River and the Hindu Kush mountains.

Bar Kokhba Literally, "Son of the Star", it is the designation of Simeon bar Kosiba, who led the Second Jewish Revolt against Rome in 132–135 CE.

Bar Kokhba Revolt The second revolt of the Jews of the Land of Israel against Rome, which took place in 132–135 CE.

Before the Common Era Abbreviated to BCE, it is an alternate designation for BC.

Belial (in the Bible and rabbinical commentary) Worthlessness, wickedness or destruction.

benediction *Ecclesiastical* The act of uttering a blessing or the advantage conferred by blessing; a mercy or benefit.

canon The authoritative corpus of Holy Scriptures.

canonisation The process by which the contents of the Holy Scriptures and, specifically, each of the sections of the Hebrew Bible, were closed and determined to be authoritative.

Common Era Abbreviated to CE, it is an alternate designation for AD.

concordance An alphabetical index of the principal words of a book, with a reference to the passage in which each occurs and usually some part of the context.

corpus Referring to a body of texts or manuscripts that have been grouped together, either in antiquity or by modern scholars.

Damascus The capital of Syria, in the south-western part; reputed to be the oldest continuously existing city in the world.

Dead Sea The lowest lake in the world, a salt lake between Israel and Jordan 394m below sea level.

Dead Sea Scrolls A collection of ancient Hebrew and Aramaic scripture manuscripts dating from the second century BCE to 70 CE, found in caves north-west of the Dead Sea.

Deuteronomy *Bible* The fifth book of the Pentateuch, containing a second statement of the Mosaic law.

Diaspora Greek for "dispersion", referring to the Jewish population outside the Land of Israel.

Edom An ancient region between the Dead Sea and the Gulf of Aqaba, bordering ancient Palestine. Greek, Idumaea or Idumea.

Ein Feshkha Agricultural settlement 3km north of Qumran, on the Dead Sea shore.

End of Days A biblical term that later Jewish tradition understood to refer to the messianic era.

Enoch *Bible* 1. The father of Methuselah (Gen. 5: 18-24). 2. The elder son of Cain (Gen. 4:17, 18).

Ephraim *Old Testament* The younger son of Joseph (Gen. 41:52).

eschatology Doctrines concerning the End of Days or the messianic era.

Essenes A sect of Jews in ancient Palestine, first appearing in second century BCE, distinguished by its withdrawal from the mainstream of society, its piety, and its ascetic ideals. Many scholars identify this group with the sect of the Dead Sea Scrolls.

Ethiopic Ancient Semitic language of Ethiopia.

exegesis Critical explanation or interpretation, especially of Scripture.

Ezekiel 1. Sixth century BCE, one of the major Hebrew prophets. 2. The 26th book of the Old Testament, written by him.

Ezra 1. Fifth century BCE, Hebrew scribe and priest who, with Nehemiah, led the revival of Judaism in Palestine. 2. A short book of chronicles of the Old Testament.

First Temple The Jerusalem Temple erected by Solomon c. 850 BCE, destroyed by the Babylonians in 586 BCE. The term can also designate the period during which this Temple stood.

Ge'ez The classical form of the ancient Ethiopic language, still used today in Ethiopian liturgy.

Gemara In Jewish literature, the later of the two sections of the Talmud, consisting of a commentary on the Mishnah.

genizah A storeroom for old Hebrew books no longer used for holy purposes. The famous Cairo *genizah* yielded up a treasure of manuscripts of Second Temple, rabbinic and medieval texts.

Great Revolt The revolt of the Jews of the Land of Israel against Rome in 66–73 CE; another term for the First Jewish Revolt.

halakhah plural halakhot That part of Jewish traditional literature concerned with the Law.

Hagiographa 1. The third of the three Jewish divisions of the Old Testament, variously arranged, but usually comprising the Psalms, Proverbs, Job, Canticles, Ruth, Lamentations, Ecclesiastes, Esther, Daniel, Ezra, Nehemiah and Chronicles. 2. Writings on saints' lives.

Ḥasidim Hebrew for "pious ones", a loosely organised group of pietists known from the Maccabean period through Mishnaic times.

Hasmonean Pertaining to the dynasty of Maccabean descendants and the period of their rule (152–63 BCE).

Hellenism The amalgamation of the Greek and native Near Eastern cultures that swept over the entire Near East in the wake of Alexander the Great's conquest.

Herodian Relating to Herod the Great (37–4 BCE), his family or its supporters.

Hillel 60 BCE–9 CE, a Pharisee of Babylonian

origin, an authority on Judaic oral tradition.

Hodayot Thanksgiving Psalms.

Israel's War of Independence Israel was established as a Jewish state in 1948.

Jubilees, Book of A more extensive rewriting of the Book of Genesis and the beginning of Exodus (through chapter 14), usually dated to the second century BCE. Twelve Qumran manuscripts of this text have been identified.

Judah 1. The fourth son of Jacob and Leah. 2. The powerful tribe of his descendants. 3. An ancient kingdom in southern Palestine, including tribes of Judah and Benjamin.

Jude A short book of the New Testament written by "a brother of James" (and possibly of Jesus).

Judaea The southern part of Palestine under the Romans.

Ketuvim See Hagiographa.

Khirbet Arabic for "ruin". The term is often used in place names in which Arabic usage preserves the name of a place that has been destroyed.

Kittim A place name in the Aegean Islands, perhaps Kition in Cyprus, that in Dead Sea Scrolls texts serves as a code word for "Romans".

late antiquity The period between the rise of Alexander the Great (c. 330 BCE) and the Muslim conquest (c. 638 CE).

Levites 1. A descendant of Levi; one of the tribe of Levi. 2. One of those who assisted the priests in the tabernacle or temple.

Leviticus The third book of the Old Testament, containing laws relating to the priests and Levites and to the forms of Jewish ceremonial observance.

Maccabean Revolt The revolt of the Jews led by the Maccabean family against the Seleucid rulers of Syria in 168–164 BCE. The victory of the Jews is celebrated on the holiday of Hanukkah.

Maccabees The family of Judah the Maccabee. The term is often used imprecisely to designate late members of the Hasmonean dynasty, as well.

Mar The equivalent of "Sir" or "Mister".

Maṣada A site on the western shore of the Dead Sea, the destruction of which brought to an end the Jewish revolt against Rome of 66–73 CE.

Masora 1. The accepted text of the Hebrew scriptures, from which variant readings and inconsistencies had gradually been excised through a succession of centuries. 2. The collection of critical notes preserving the tradition.

Masorete One of the body of Jewish scholars who reduced the Masora to writing.

Masoretic Text The traditional, authoritative Hebrew text of the Bible, considered as such by Jews from mishnaic times until the present. The term derives from "*mesorah*", tradition.

Memphis Ancient capital of Egypt; now a ruined city in Upper Egypt, on the Nile, south of Cairo.

Menasheh One of the sons of Jacob.

Metropolitan *Ecclesiastical* Denoting chief priest of high rank, a bishop.

mezuzah *plural* **mezuzot** A manuscript of specific biblical verses – affirming God's sovereignty over the world and the obligation to observe his Law – that is affixed to the doorpost of a Jewish home in accord with the command of the Torah.

millenarian Of or relating to a thousand, especially the thousand years of the prophesised millennium.

millennium *Bible* The period of "a thousand years" (a phrase variously interpreted) during which Christ is to reign on earth, according to the prophetic statement in Rev. 20:1–7.

Mishmarot The 24 courses into which the Jewish priests were divided. The courses were the subject of various Qumran texts that, while setting out the schedule for officiating in the Temple, set forth the solar calendar proposed by the sect and related groups.

Mishnah The great collection of early rabbinic law edited by Rabbi Judah the Prince (135–220 CE). The term can also designate a particular paragraph of that code.

monotheism The doctrine or belief that there is only one god.

Nahum 1. A Hebrew prophet of the late seventh century BCE. 2. A book of the Old Testament, the seventh among the Minor Prophets.

Near East An indefinite geographical or regional term, referring to the Balkan States, Egypt and the countries of south-western Asia.

Nevi'im See the Prophets.

New Testament Those books in the Bible that were produced by the early Christian Church and added to the Old Testament (the Jewish Scriptures).

Nineveh The ancient capital of Assyria; its ruins are opposite Mosul, on the river Tigris, in northern Iraq.

Old Testament 1. The collection of biblical books comprising the Hebrew Scriptures of "the old convenant", and being the first of the two main divisions of the Christian bible. 2. The convenant between God and Israel on Mount Sinai, constituting the basis of the Hebrew religion.

oral law A second Torah (law), consisting of interpretations of the written Torah, which was studied and passed down by oral tradition. In rabbinic Judaism, this oral Torah, believed to have been given by God at Sinai along with the written Torah, constitutes the authoritative interpretation of the written law.

ordinance 1. An authoritative rule or law; a decree or command. 2. A public injunction or regulation. 3. *Ecclesiastical* a) an established rule or ceremony; b) a sacrament; c) the communion.

ossuary A place or receptacle for the bones of the dead.

ostracon *plural* **ostraca** A piece of broken pottery (a potsherd) used in antiquity for the writing of short texts or quick notes.

palaeo- A prefix meaning old, ancient.

palaeography The study of the shapes of letters and their history, usually to facilitate the dating of inscriptions and manuscripts.

Pentateuch The first five books of the Bible, also termed the Torah, or the Five Books of Moses.

pesher *plural* **pesharim** The unique biblical interpretations and commentaries of the Dead Sea sect, which understood the words of the biblical prophets as referring to the experiences of sectarians in the Second Temple period.

Pharisees A group of Jews in Second Temple times who constituted the spiritual forebears of the talmudic rabbis. Led by lay teachers of the Torah, they became the dominant sect. The word derives from Hebrew *perushim*, "separate".

Phoenicia An ancient maritime country on the east coast of the Mediterranean Sea.

the Prophets The books which form the second of the three Jewish divisions of the Old Testament, comprising a. Joshua, Judges, I and II Samuel, and I and II Kings; b. Isaiah, Jeremiah, and Ezekiel (Major Prophets); c. Hosea, Joel, Amos, Obadiah, Jonah, Micah, Nahum, Habakkuk, Zephaniah, Haggai, Zechariah, and Malachi (Minor Prophets). Group a. is called the Former Prophets; groups b. and c. together the Latter Prophets.

phylacteries Cubical compartments of leather

that contain biblical passages emphasising God's sovereignty and the obligation of the Jews to observe His commandments, which are affixed to the head and arm with leather thongs. They are known in Hebrew as *tefillin*.

pietistic Depth of religious feeling; godliness of life.

Prayer for King Jonathan This manuscript, of which only a fragment survives, has both an excerpt from one of the Apocryphal psalms contained in the Psalms Scroll and a prayer for the welfare of a King Jonathan, whom most scholars have identified as Alexander Jannaeus, the Hasmonean ruler (104–76 BCE).

pseudepigrapha Literally, referring to books written in the Hellenistic age in the name of an ancient biblical figure. Generally, the term is used to designate much of the religious literature of the various groups within Second Temple Judaism.

Ptolemies The rulers of Egypt and its empire in the Hellenistic era.

Qumran (Khirbet Qumran) A site on the western shore of the Dead Sea. The Dead Sea Scrolls were uncovered in nearby caves. Qumran itself preserves the ruins of a building complex, which purportedly served as the headquarters of the sect in the Second Temple period.

rabbi Hebrew for "my master, my teacher", referring to the teachers and judges of the Jews of Palestine in the Roman and Byzantine periods. The rabbis who shaped the texts of talmudic Judaism are collectively termed "the Rabbis".

rabbinic Hebrew The Hebrew language as used by the rabbis in their writings; the later Hebrew.

ritual 1. An established or prescribed procedure, code, etc, for a religious or other rite. 2. A form or system of religious or other rites. 3. Observances or set forms in public worship. 4. A book of rites or ceremonies. 5. Any solemn or customary action, code of behaviour, etc, regulating social conduct.

Sabbath The seventh day of the week (Saturday) as the day of rest and observance among the Jews.

Sabbatical The designation for every seventh year, in which the Bible commands the remission of debts and prescribes leaving the land fallow.

Sadducees A sect of Second Temple period Jews, connected primarily with the priestly aristocracy, which accepted only the authority of teachings based strictly on the Bible and its interpretation. The word derives from "Zadok", the high priest in the time of Solomon.

Samaritan The Aramaic dialect spoken in Samaria, the northern kingdom of the ancient Hebrews, in Palestine, between the river Jordan and the Mediterranean Sea.

Samaritans A mixed people inhabiting certain parts of the Land of Israel, descended from those original northern Israelites who were not exiled in 722 BCE and the tribes introduced into the area by the Assyrians.

sara^cat A disease of the skin that is normally mistranslated in English Bibles as "leprosy". (Leprosy is a disease with much more permanent and more serious symptoms.)

scall A scaly or scabby disease of the skin, especially of the scalp.

scriptorium A room in a monastery set apart for the writing or copying of manuscripts.

Second Temple The Jerusalem Temple that was in use from 520 BCE until its destruction by the Romans in 70 CE. The term can also designate the period during which this Temple stood.

sect *adjective* **sectarian** The terms designate the various groups of Jews and their particular approaches to Judaism in Second Temple times. Such usage does not imply that any one of the groups is to be considered a mainstream.

Seleucids The dynasty that ruled Syria in Hellenistic times.

Septuagint The Greek translation of the Old Testament produced in Egypt in the Hellenistic period, said to have been made at the request of Ptolemy II, by 72 Jewish scholars, in 72 days.

serekh A list of laws or regulations compiled by the Dead Sea sect as part of its regular formal study sessions.

Six Day War A war fought for six days in June 1967 in which Israel defeated Egypt, Jordan and Syria and occupied the Gaza Strip, the Sinai, Jerusalem, the West Bank and the Golan Heights.

solander A box, especially one for botanical specimens (and paper artefacts), made in the form of a book, the cover being the lid.

Syriac A dialect of Aramaic, now only in liturgical use.

tabernacle 1. (usually cap) The tent used by the Jews as a portable sanctuary before their final settlement in Palestine. 2. Any place of worship, especially one designed for a large congregation.

Talmud *adjective* **talmudic** Referring to the Mishnah and Gemara, the literary results of the rabbinic discussions of Jewish law and tradition. Talmudic Judaism is that defined by the rabbis in the first two centuries CE and further expounded until the end of the fifth century.

Targum Aramaic translations of the Hebrew biblical books.

"Teacher of Righteousness" A sectarian leader who was apparently active soon after the founding of the Dead Sea sect. It is possible there was a series of teachers who filled this role.

tefillin See phylacteries.

Tetragrammaton The four-lettered name of God, YHVH (or JHVH, JHWH, YHWH). Already in late antiquity this name was not pronounced because of the great reverence in which it was held. It was therefore also called "the ineffable name".

Torah The Five Books of Moses, the Pentateuch. The Hebrew word "*torah*" literally means "instruction, teaching".

transliterate To change (letters, words, etc) into corresponding characters of another alphabet or language.

Tyre An ancient seaport of Phoenicia; one of the great cities of antiquity, famous for its navigators and traders on the same site.

vac A space left intentionally by the scribe.

wadi 1. The channel of a watercourse which is dry except during periods of rainfall. 2. The stream or watercourse itself.

"Wicked Priest" A Hasmonean priestly leader seen by the sect as its arch enemy. This priest apparently had a confrontation with the Qumran "Teacher of Righteousness".

yaḥad The group within the Judaean Desert sect who chose to live communally.

Zadok *adjective* **Zadokite** Zadok was one of the high priests of King Solomon in the tenth century BCE. His Zadokite priestly line dominated the high priesthood for most of Jewish history.

Zion 1. A hill or mount of Jerusalem, the site of the temple. 2. The Israelites. 3. The Jewish people. 4. Israel as the national home of the Jews. 5. The theocracy, or Church of God. 6. Heaven as the final gathering place of true believers.

CONTRIBUTORS

Ruth Peled is Director of Special Projects, Israel Antiquities Authority, and Co-curator of the *Dead Sea Scrolls* exhibition.

Ayala Sussmann is Director of Publications, Israel Antiquities Authority, and Co-curator of the *Dead Sea Scrolls* exhibition.

Donald T. Ariel is Curator of Numismatics, Israel Antiquities Authority.

Tamar Schick is Curator of Organic Materials, Israel Antiquities Authority.

Pnina Shor is Head of the Department of Artefacts' Treatment and Conservation, Israel Antiquities Authority.

Michael E. Stone is Professor of Comparative Religion and Armenian Studies, The Hebrew University of Jerusalem.

Emanuel Tov is Professor of Biblical Literature, The Hebrew University of Jerusalem, and Editor-in-chief of the Dead Sea Scrolls Publication Project, Israel Antiquities Authority.

Ada Yardeni is Research Fellow in Palaeography, The Hebrew University of Jerusalem.

SELECTED BIBLIOGRAPHY

OFFICIAL SERIES

***Discoveries in the Judaean Desert (DJD)*, Clarendon Press, Oxford, 1955– .**

Vol. I: Barthélemy, D., and Milik, J.T., 1955, *Qumran Cave 1*.

Vol. II: Benoit, P., Milik, J.T., and de Vaux, R., 1961, *Les Grottes de Murabba'ât*.

Vol. III: Baillet, M., Milik, J.T., and de Vaux, R., 1962, *Les "Petites Grottes" de Qumran*.

Vol. IV: Sanders, J.A., 1965, *The Psalms Scroll of Qumran Cave 11 (11QPsª)*.

Vol. V: Allegro, J.M., 1968, *Qumran Cave 4: I (4Q158–4Q186)*.

Vol. VI: de Vaux, R., and Milik, J.T., 1977, *Qumran Grotte 4: II (Archéologie et 4Q128–4Q157)*.

Vol. VII: Baillet, M., 1982, *Qumran Grotte 4: III (4Q482–4Q520)*.

Vol. VIII: Tov, E., 1990, *The Greek Minor Prophets Scroll from Naḥal Ḥever (8HevXIIgr) (The Seiyâl Collection I)*.

Vol. IX: Skehan, P., Ulrich, E., and Sanderson, J., 1992, *Qumran Cave 4: IV. Paleo-Hebrew and Greek Biblical Manuscripts*, with a contribution by P.J. Parsons.

Vol. X: Qimron, E., and Strugnell, J., 1994, *Qumran Cave 4: V. Miqsat Ma'ase ha-Torah*.

Vol. XI: Eshel, E., et al, 1998, *Qumran Cave 4: VI. Poetical and Liturgical Texts, Part I*.

Vol. XII: Ulrich, E., and Cross, F.M. (eds), 1994, *Qumran Cave 4: VII. Genesis to Numbers*.

Vol. XIII: Attridge, H., et al, 1994, *Qumran Cave 4: VIII. Parabiblical Texts, Part I*.

Vol. XIV: Ulrich, E., and Cross, F.M. (eds), 1995, *Qumran Cave 4: IX. Deuteronomy, Joshua, Judges, Kings*.

Vol. XV: Ulrich, E. (ed.), 1997, *Qumran Cave 4: X. The Prophets*.

Vol. XVIII: Baumgarten, J.M., 1996, *Qumran Cave 4: XIII. The Damascus Document (4Q266–4Q273)*.

Vol. XIX: Broshi, M., et al, 1995, *Qumran Cave 4: XIV. Parabiblical Texts, Part 2*.

Vol. XX: Elgvin, T., et al, 1997, *Qumran Cave 4: XV. Sapiential Texts, Part I*.

Vol. XXII: Brooke, G., et al, 1996, *Qumran Cave 4: XVII. Parabiblical Texts, Part 3*.

Vol. XXIII: García-Martínez, F., Tigchelaar, E.J.C., and van der Woude, A.S., 1998, *Qumran Cave 11: II. 11Q2–18, 11Q20–30*.

Vol. XXIV: Leith, M.J.W., 1997, *The Wadi Daliyeh Seal Impressions*.

Vol. XXV: Puech, E., 1998, *Qumran Cave 4: XVIII. Textes Hébreux*.

Vol. XXVI: Alexander, P.S., and Vermes, G., 1998, *Qumran Cave 4: XIX. 4Q Serekh ha-Yahad and Two Related Texts*.

Vol. XXVII: Cotton, H.M., and Yardeni, A., 1997, *Aramaic, Hebrew, and Greek Documentary Texts from Naḥal Hever and other Sites (The Seiyâl Collection II)*.

Vol. XXIX: Chazon, E., et al, 1999, *Qumran Cave 4: XX. Poetical and Liturgical Texts, Part 2*.

Vol. XXXIV: Strugnell, J., et al, 1999, *Qumran Cave 4: XXIV. Sapiential Texts, Part 2*.

Vol. XXXV: Baumgarten, J., et al, 1999, *Qumran Cave 4: XXV. Halakhic Texts*.

GENERAL SOURCES

Boccaccini, G., 1998, *Beyond the Essene Hypothesis: The Parting of the Ways between Qumran and Enochic Judaism*, Eerdmans, Grand Rapids.

Charlesworth, J.H. (ed.), 1992, *Jesus and the Dead Sea Scrolls*, Crossroads, New York.

Collins, J., 1997, *Apocalypticism in the Dead Sea Scrolls*, Routledge, London.

Cross, F.M., 1995, "The Development of the Jewish Scripts", in *The Bible and the Ancient Near East: Essays in Honor of William Foxwell Albright*, revised edition, edited by G.E. Wright, Doubleday, New York.

De Vaux, R., 1973, *Archaeology and the Dead Sea Scrolls*, Oxford University Press, Oxford.

Dimant, D., and Rappaport, U. (eds), 1992, *The Dead Sea Scrolls: Forty Years of Research*, Brill, Leiden.

Dimant, D., and Rappaport, U. (eds), 1996, *The Ancient Library of Qumran* (3rd edn), Fortress Press, Minneapolis.

Fitzmyer, J., 1992, *Responses to 101 Questions on the Dead Sea Scrolls*, Paulist Press, New York.

Flint, P.W., and Vanderkam, J.C. (eds), 1998, *The Dead Sea Scrolls After Fifty Years: A Comprehensive Assessment*, Brill, Leiden.

García-Martínez, F., 1997, *The Dead Sea Scrolls Translated* (2nd edn), Brill, Leiden.

Kugel, J., 1995, *The Bible as It Was*, Harvard University Press, Cambridge.

Roitman, A. (ed.), 1997, *A Day at Qumran: The Dead Sea Sect and Its Scrolls*, The Israel Museum, Jerusalem.

Schechter, S., 1970, *Documents of Jewish Sectaries*, first published in 1910, Library of Biblical Studies, KTAV Press, New York.

Schiffman, L.H., 1996, *Reclaiming the Dead Sea Scrolls*, Jewish Publication Society, Philadelphia.

Shanks, H. (ed.), 1992, *Understanding the Dead Sea Scrolls: A Reader from the Biblical Archaeological Review*, Random House, New York.

Stegemann, H., 1998, *The Library of Qumran: On the Essenes, Qumran, John the Baptist and Jesus*, Eerdmans, Grand Rapids.

Talmon, S., 1995, "A Calendrical Document from Qumran Cave 4 (*Mishmarot D, 4Q325*)", in *Solving Riddles and*

Untying Knots: Studies in Honor of Jonas C. Greenfield, edited by Z. Zevit, et al, Winona Lake, Indiana, pp. 327–344.

Tov, E., 1997, "Tefillin of Different Origin from Qumran", in *A Light for Jacob*, edited by H. Hoffman and F.W. Polak, Bialik Institute, Jerusalem.

Ulrich, E., 1999, *The Dead Sea Scrolls and the Origin of the Bible*, Eerdmans, Grand Rapids.

Vanderkam, J., 1994, *The Dead Sea Scrolls Today*, Eerdmans, Grand Rapids.

Vanderkam, J., 1998, *Calendars in the Dead Sea Scrolls: Measuring Time*, Routledge, London.

Vermes, G., 1997, *The Complete Dead Sea Scrolls in English* (5th edn), Penguin, New York.

TRANSCRIPTIONS, REPRODUCTIONS AND RECONSTRUCTIONS

• *The Dead Sea Scrolls on Microfiche: A Comprehensive Facsimile Edition of the Texts from the Judaean Desert*, 1993, edited by E. Tov, printed catalogue by S. Reed, Israel Antiquities Authority, Brill, Leiden.

• *A Facsimile Edition of the Dead Sea Scrolls*, 1991, prepared with an introduction and index by R. Eisenman and J. Robinson, in 2 volumes, Biblical Archaeology Society, Washington, DC.

• *A Preliminary Edition of the Unpublished Dead Sea Scrolls: The Hebrew and Aramaic Texts from Cave Four*, 1991–92, reconstructed and edited by B. Wacholder and M. Abegg, 2 fascs, Biblical Archaeology Society, Washington, DC.

• *The Scroll of the War of the Sons of Light Against the Sons of Darkness*, 1962, edited by Y. Yadin, translated by B. and C. Rabin, Oxford University Press, Oxford.

• *Scrolls from Qumran Cave I. The Great Isaiah Scroll, the Order of the Community, the Pesher to Habakkuk*, 1972, with photographs by J. Trever, Albright Institute of Archaeological Research and the Shrine of the Book, Jerusalem.

• *The Temple Scroll*, 1977–83, edited by Y. Yadin, in 3 volumes, Israel Exploration Society, Jerusalem, Israel.

THERE SHALL BE BUILT THE ROYAL TEMPLE OF THE GREAT ONE

N HIS GLORIOUS SPLENDOUR, FOR ALL GENERATIONS FOR EVER

ENOCH

מגילות ים המלח